The
Motivated
Student

Unlocking the Enthusiasm for Learning

Bob Sullo

D1166241

ASCD

Alexandria, Virginia USA

1703 N. Beauregard St. • Alexandria, VA 22311-1714 USA
Phone: 800-933-2723 or 703-578-9600 • Fax: 703-575-5400
Web site: www.ascd.org • E-mail: member@ascd.org
Author guidelines: www.ascd.org/write

Gene R. Carter, *Executive Director*; Nancy Modrak, *Publisher*; Julie Houtz, *Director of Book Editing & Production*; Ernesto Yermoli, *Project Manager*; Cathy Guyer, *Senior Graphic Designer*; Mike Kalyan, *Production Manager*; Valerie Younkin, *Desktop Publishing Specialist*; Kyle Steichen, *Production Specialist*

Printed in the United States of America. Cover art copyright © 2009 by ASCD. ASCD publications present a variety of viewpoints. The views expressed or implied in this book should not be interpreted as official positions of the Association.

All Web links in this book are correct as of the publication date below but may have become inactive or otherwise modified since that time. If you notice a deactivated or changed link, please e-mail books@ascd.org with the words "Link Update" in the subject line. In your message, please specify the Web link, the book title, and the page number on which the link appears.

PAPERBACK ISBN: 978-1-4166-0810-3   ASCD product #109028   n6/09

Also available as an e-book through ebrary, netLibrary, and many online booksellers (see Books in Print for the ISBNs).

Quantity discounts for the paperback edition only: 10–49 copies, 10%; 50+ copies, 15%; for 1,000 or more copies, call 800-933-2723, ext. 5634, or 703-575-5634. For desk copies: member@ascd.org.

Library of Congress Cataloging-in-Publication Data
Sullo, Robert A., 1951–
    The motivated student : unlocking the enthusiasm for learning / Bob Sullo.
        p. cm.
    Includes bibliographical references and index.
    ISBN 978-1-4166-0810-3 (pbk. : alk. paper)
    1. Motivation in education.   2. Effective teaching.   3. Teacher–student relationships.
I. Title.

    LB1065.S865 2009
    370.15′4—dc22

                                                                2009005850

20 19 18 17 16 15 14 13 12 11 10   2 3 4 5 6 7 8 9 10 11 12

For Kristy, Greg, & Melanie.

You should be very proud of yourselves!

The Motivated Student

Unlocking the Enthusiasm for Learning

Acknowledgments

Substantive, enthusiastic conversation about education helps clarify my thinking as I write. I had numerous fruitful discussions with colleagues I respect as I worked on this book. Although I no doubt will unintentionally neglect to mention everyone who helped, I am especially grateful to the following people for sharing their thoughts, insights, and questions: John Erwin, author of *The Classroom of Choice*; Sue Tomaszewski of Orleans/Niagara BOCES; Ruth Mitchell and Linda Radtke of High Schools That Work, Southwest Ohio; Erika Brockman, Turi Nilsson, and the entire staff of Southwest Baltimore Charter School; and Craig White and Marcy Emberger of Atlantic Canada Connected Community.

A special thanks goes to Scott Willis, ASCD's director of Book Acquisitions and Development. Throughout the submission process, Scott provided valuable feedback and guidance. His support and belief in this book were unwavering.

I was fortunate to once again work with Ernesto Yermoli, who served as the project manager for this book. Ernesto has the ability to clarify and simplify what I write without compromising the content. Thanks to Ernesto, readers have a tighter, better book in their hands.

And finally, thank you to my wife Laurie, who gives me the time and space I need when I get "lost" in writing.

Introduction

In the past quarter-century, we have seen the emergence of numerous "best practices" that have significantly improved curriculum and instruction. A sampling of innovations includes differentiated instruction, Understanding by Design, the emergence of state standards, the development of curriculum frameworks, scope-and-sequence charts that inform teachers of what to teach and when to teach it, the expanded use of technology in education, active literacy, curriculum mapping, and the proliferation of professional learning communities. Formative assessment informs instruction like never before. In short, teaching has become significantly more "professional."

That said, our schools are still in trouble—big trouble. Christopher Swanson, the director of the Editorial Projects in Education Research Center, states: "When 30 percent of our ninth-graders (ultimately) fail to finish high school with a diploma, we are dealing with a crisis that has frightening implications for our ... future" (Chaddock, 2006). The dropout rate in urban areas is even higher; the situation, even more grim.

What about those who remain in school? In *Results Now*, Mike Schmoker (2006) reports the following alarming statistic based on 1,500 classroom observations: in 85 percent of the classrooms observed, fewer than half of the students were paying attention!

Despite exemplary innovations in curriculum and instruction, students are dropping out of school at an alarming rate, and many of those who remain don't seem to be paying attention. How can we explain this discrepancy? Educational advances have focused on curriculum and instruction, the *what* and *how* of teaching. Far less attention has been paid to the *who* of teaching: the students. While we have developed ingenious methods to teach what we think is most important, we have largely ignored those toward whom we are supposed to be directing our effort.

We pay scant attention to students because we believe we know what motivates them; we are confident that if we appropriately reward and reinforce desired behavior, the students will thrive. Clearly, however, this is not the case. Nevertheless, the outmoded reward/punishment paradigm, which is still tightly woven into the most laudable attempts to improve curriculum and instruction, continues to wield a stranglehold on our thinking. More and more schools pay students for increased academic achievement, the ultimate "carrot and stick" strategy. According to the *Washington Post*, schools in Washington, D.C., New York City, Chicago, Baltimore, and Boston have all recently initiated programs that provide money and other tangible rewards to students for good grades and improved behavior (Turque, 2008). A review of our current best practices will find very few voices arguing vigorously against the notion that we can externally motivate students to achieve academically with the right blend of positive reinforcement and unpleasant sanctions. This book is different.

The Motivated Student: Unlocking the Enthusiasm for Learning is based on the premise that our ideas about motivation are wrongheaded and that practices based on this flawed model unintentionally limit student achievement. As long as we continue to organize our educational practices around reward and punishment, we will see high dropout rates and a student body that is alarmingly inattentive. Once we structure schools and classrooms around the idea that students are internally motivated, we will be able to take full advantage of the many recent innovations and advances in curriculum and instruction.

In *The Quality School* (1990), Dr. William Glasser defines teaching as a "process of imparting knowledge through a variety of techniques ... to people who want to acquire this knowledge" (pp. 174–175). Using Glasser's definition, *we don't have a teaching problem!* The heart of the matter is the relative clause "who want to acquire this knowledge." Given students who want to learn what we are trying to teach, ideas about curriculum and instruction are put to good use. Teacher preparation programs have improved dramatically in these areas, and teachers today are well prepared to effectively teach those "who want to acquire this knowledge." The staggering dropout rate and number of students who do not pay attention in class are sobering indicators that not enough students are positively engaged in the learning process. Too many drop out or become "enrolled dropouts," those who remain on class rosters but are disengaged and unmotivated.

While concerted efforts to improve curriculum and instruction have largely eradicated widespread teaching problems, the harsh reality is that good teaching is not enough. In addition to teaching, we need to effectively *manage*, which is defined by Glasser (1990) as "the process of convincing people that working hard and doing a quality job of what the teacher asks them to do will add quality to their lives" (p. 176). Students who see achieving, working hard, and doing what we ask as enhancing their lives are less likely to drop out and more likely to be attentive and engaged when they are in our classes.

The Motivated Student provides a concrete approach to engaging students through effective management, the missing piece in the achievement puzzle. It offers strategies to incorporate into your repertoire as well as practices to avoid. You will encounter teachers from across grade levels who put these strategies into practice every day. The situations and conversations in this book represent both "real" stories and composites woven together to illustrate a particular point. For that reason, the names of teachers and students are fictitious.

Begin by reading the book in its entirety. Then choose a particular strategy you want to incorporate into your teaching. Go back to that chapter to study what the teacher did to engage the students. Determine how you can implement the same principles in a way that matches your style and your personality and is appropriate to the students, subject, and grade level you teach. Some chapters describe teachers who engage in practices that diminish student engagement and learning. You can also learn from these chapters by reviewing them and honestly assessing whether you engage in some of those same practices. Enhance your teaching by developing alternative approaches that inspire your students.

After you become comfortable, choose another strategy, and then another, until you have woven all of the strategies presented here into your repertoire. The more strategies you implement, the more engaged your students will be, the less disruption you will face, the greater achievement you will inspire, and the greater satisfaction you will derive from teaching.

Although failures in education persist, they need not go on forever. After all, there is something fundamentally "natural" about teaching. When caring adults with expertise pass on valuable information and skills to the next generation, it can be—and should be—a joyful experience. We can only take full advantage of the array of the best practices that have been developed when we simultaneously implement strategies that engage and inspire our students.

Eliminate Fear
from the Classroom

Despite compelling evidence to the contrary, many teachers still believe that fear—fear of failure, fear of an unwanted call home, fear of the teacher, fear of ridicule, or fear of an unpleasant consequence—is a prime motivator for students to do high-quality work. The intentional creation of fear in the classroom remains one of the most widely used strategies for managing student behavior and encouraging academic achievement.

But fear compromises our ability to learn. In this chapter, you will meet a well-intentioned teacher who undermines his capacity to inspire high achievement by creating a classroom environment infused with fear.

Mr. Lewiston

As students filed into Sam Lewiston's fourth-period U.S. History class, the first thing that struck me was that they were relatively quiet. By midmorning, most high school juniors are an energized, if not boisterous, group. These students were remarkably subdued, quickly taking their seats and opening their notebooks even before the bell rang. It was evident that no one wanted to be caught unprepared for the beginning of class.

At the front of the room, Mr. Lewiston reviewed his notes and the day's agenda, posted on the whiteboard along with two quotations:

"There are no gains without pains." —Benjamin Franklin

"Feel the fear and do it anyway." —Susan Jeffers

The bell rang, and Mr. Lewiston closed the door. Seconds later, two students entered sheepishly. One started to explain that there had been some congestion in the hall, but he was quickly silenced by Mr. Lewiston.

"Caleb, you know the rules. Don't aggravate the situation with a pointless plea. I'll see you this afternoon. Same with you, Trevor."

The two students took their seats as classmates traded nervous glances. Mr. Lewiston calmly wrote the names of the two students on the board under the heading "Detention."

"Okay, let's begin. We have a major exam tomorrow. While the stakes are high for every one of you, some of you are currently failing, and your performance tomorrow will go a long way in determining if you pass or fail this quarter. I won't embarrass any of you by announcing who you are. You know if this pertains to you." As Mr. Lewiston made this pronouncement, he looked around the room, letting his gaze settle on a half-dozen students who worked furiously to avert eye contact.

"I'm pleased to add that some of you are doing quite well," Mr. Lewiston continued, "but remember that one poor grade can negate what you have done thus far. Now is not the time to relax. Tomorrow's test will be fair. It will also be challenging, to say the least."

The bulk of the class period was spent reviewing a study guide for the upcoming test. Mr. Lewiston's pace was brisk. He called on students randomly. Those who were unable to provide an answer within a few seconds were admonished with comments like, "Earth to Alicia. Wake up. Test tomorrow," and "Armand, your lack of preparation never ceases to amaze me." A few students smiled nervously, but most kept their eyes glued to their notebooks and study guides. When students provided correct answers, Mr. Lewiston acknowledged their success but reminded them, "It's how you do in the game that matters. This is practice. Tomorrow is the big game. Don't let up."

With one minute remaining, Mr. Lewiston said, "Kindly put away your study guides, close your notebooks, and give me your full attention. Tomorrow's test will be an important determinant in the grade you receive this quarter. I encourage each of you to remember the stakes, prepare to the best of your ability, and prove that you want to be successful by doing well on tomorrow's test. Caleb and Trevor, remember your detention this afternoon." With that, the bell rang, and students filed out of the room as quietly and orderly as they had entered it.

The Students' Perspective

I had a chance to catch up with several students from the class later that day. I asked about their impressions of their teacher, his style, and his class.

"Well, it's pretty obvious he's kind of a no-nonsense hard-ass," began Caleb, one of the students assigned to detention.

"Is he fair?" I asked.

"Absolutely," answered Caleb. "That's what makes it semitolerable. I knew when I walked into class like two seconds late that I was going to get a detention. I'm not even sure why I tried to explain that it was crowded in the halls. No matter what you say, it's not going to change anything. Mr. Lewiston has his rules, they're nonnegotiable, and that's the end of that story."

"Seriously!" exclaimed Marcy, a girl who had correctly answered several questions during the class I had observed. "I remember one time being late because I was talking with my Spanish teacher. Even though I had a pass from her, Mr. Lewiston still gave me a detention. When I complained, he just said to me, 'Marcy, your Spanish teacher cannot excuse you from my detention. A pass with her signature is not a license to violate my rules.' But Caleb's right. Mr. Lewiston is fair. He would never play favorites. I mean, you heard him in class today. He doesn't just scare students who are in danger of failing. He intimidates and scares everyone!"

"Does he scare you?" I asked.

"Of course he does. Isn't it obvious? Most of us spend the class trying to avoid being singled out. To be honest, if you do your work and you're prepared, you can get through most classes without much of a problem. But a surprise attack can come at any time. That's why I just try to fly under the radar in that class," said Marcy.

"Are you a good student?" I asked Marcy.

"As of today I am," she answered with a slight smile. "But as Mr. Lewiston reminded us, that could change tomorrow."

"Do reminders that things could change for the worse keep you focused and on your toes?"

"I don't think so. I mean, in my other classes I stay on top of things, and I don't have this big cloud of fear hanging over me, so I'm not more conscientious because I'm constantly scared my grade will drop. I do know that I would never say anything controversial or risky in that class. It's just easier—and way smarter—to follow the script and move on with minimal damage."

"Anyone want to add anything else?" I asked.

"I've got something," offered Armand. "I think if you ask most kids, they'd say Mr. Lewiston is an OK guy. I mean, he makes sarcastic comments like he made to me today about not being prepared, but he's not trying to be nasty. It's just his way of motivating us. I think he believes if we're not constantly afraid of imminent doom and failure, we'll do less. Even when he's being critical, most kids don't feel that he's the enemy or anything. He's just thinks his job is to instill fear."

"So his style is OK with most students," I said.

"Oh, no!" the students exclaimed in chorus. "It's a struggle to get through his class. You live in constant fear that you'll be zapped and humiliated. A good day in Mr. Lewiston's class is when you remain invisible."

"One last question," I said. "Anyone here planning to go to college and major in history?"

"Now that," said Caleb, "is one of the funniest things I've ever heard!"

Mr. Lewiston's Teaching Philosophy

When I arrived at Sam Lewiston's room that afternoon for our follow-up conversation, he immediately stood up, shook my hand,

and asked if I wanted anything to eat or drink. The contrast between how he treated me and how he managed his students was so glaring that it deserved mention.

"Whole different atmosphere and approach in here," I ventured.

"Absolutely," said Sam, a grin spreading across his face. "You and I are colleagues having a conversation about something I love: teaching. When you saw me earlier today, I was wearing my teacher hat. There are specific things I need to do and ways I need to act with my students if I'm to have the success I want."

"Tell me about that," I encouraged. "It sounds interesting."

"Sure," said Sam. "When I said I was wearing my teacher hat, I don't mean that I wasn't being genuine. I was. When I'm in the teacher role, my job is to make sure the kids learn as much as possible. To do that, I need to engender a healthy fear: fear of me, fear of failure, fear of an unknown future. Fear is a great motivator; without injecting it into my classroom, I wouldn't be doing my job."

"The students clearly fear you. It was palpable in the classroom today, and my subsequent conversation with a few students confirmed that they certainly experience fear."

"As strange as it may sound," Sam replied, "that's good to hear. If they weren't afraid, they'd be less motivated. I am curious, though. In your observation or conversations with students, was there any mention of fairness? Was I seen as too emotional or angry?"

"The students acknowledged your fairness and obviously appreciate it. They told me that you are tough and instill fear in them but never play favorites. And there was no mention of any emotionalism or anger."

"Good. I try to keep the emotion out of my teaching. I want to take a matter-of-fact, 'this is what happens here' approach. Like this morning, when I assigned detention to those two boys who were late to class. Nice boys, both of them. But I have rules, and there are consequences for violating those rules. At the same time, I never want to come across like I'm emotionally distressed by their behavior. They chose to be late. I invoked the sanction. Everyone in the room gets a wake-up call, and we move on."

I was struck by Sam's easygoing manner. He seemed to truly enjoy teaching and wanted what was best for his students. At the same time, his classroom was devoid of joy and laced with fear. "What about your use of sarcasm?" I asked.

"It's just another tool in my toolbox," Sam replied. Referring to his comments from earlier that day, he said, "Alicia is a nice girl, but she zones out and needs a jolt to reel her in. And Armand is a capable young man who has slid by on his native intelligence rather than developing a strong work ethic and sense of responsibility. He needs to hear that in the most unambiguous way."

"Fair enough," I countered. "But are you worried that your sarcastic comments will do more harm than good?"

"Not really," Sam answered. "These are adolescents; they trash-talk with each other routinely. My little sarcastic jabs just get their attention. More subtle forms of communication are lost on most of them. I'm sure it does no harm."

"Does it bother you to 'play the heavy' with kids?" I asked.

"Not in the least. My objective is to get kids to perform, and the simple truth is they wouldn't perform as well if I didn't hold their feet to the fire. You saw the quotations on my board. Fear and pain are essential to success, and I want success—for my students and for me. If I were to adopt a different approach, I might find my classes more enjoyable, but I would sacrifice the satisfaction I get every day knowing that I am helping my students experience academic success."

Commentary

There are teachers who feel that they must create a fear-laden environment to be successful. Sam and others of his ilk are well intentioned in their approach, in that they are driven by their desire to be as effective as possible. They truly believe that fear is a necessary component of successful learning.

My conversations with Sam and his students clearly illustrated that Sam has the best interests of the students at heart. As Armand told me, "Mr. Lewiston is an OK guy.... It's just his way of motivating us." When Sam was not in his "teacher role," his kindness and commitment to education were evident. The vast majority of teachers like Sam who intentionally create fear in the classroom do so because they believe such an atmosphere inspires academic achievement. But does it?

Let's examine the impact of fear on learning. When we feel threatened and experience fear, we downshift to survival mode. Students are less able to learn effectively because their primary focus is on self-protection. As the students told me, a good day in Sam Lewiston's class is defined by one's ability to "remain invisible."

Fear activates the well-known fight-or-flight mechanism. This autonomic physiological process sends increased amounts of oxygenated blood to the large extremities so that we are prepared to fight or flee. Because we have a finite amount of blood, the increase in blood flow to our arms and legs leads to a corresponding *decrease* in blood flow in other areas—specifically, the brain. Physiologically speaking, students in an environment characterized by fear are not able to think as effectively and learn as much as those who are in an environment that feels safe and secure.

Erik Jensen states, "Start by removing threats from the learning environment. No matter how excited you are about adding positives to the environment, first work to eliminate the negatives.... There is no evidence that threats are an effective way to meet long-term academic goals" (1998, p. 30).

One of the "tools" Sam discussed with me was his use of sarcasm. Even if Sam is right in his belief that adolescents routinely "trash-talk" with each other, there is no place for sarcasm in the repertoire of any teacher. Unfortunately, sarcastic comments remain a staple in the management approach of many teachers. Like Sam, these teachers probably believe that their sarcasm "does no harm" and is necessary to get the attention of their students. But sarcasm affects students' sense of well-being and confidence in themselves. Some students will try to "even the score" by disrupting the class and interfering with the learning process. Others will shut down and disengage. Either way, effective teaching and learning are compromised by the use of sarcasm.

Learning can be a scary process. Whenever we take on the

challenge of acquiring new knowledge or developing new skills, we make ourselves vulnerable. We are moving from a place of competence into uncharted territory. As adults, we are keenly aware of how difficult it is to leave our comfort zones. We speak glibly about the discomfort we experience during the "steep learning curve" that is part and parcel of each new learning experience. We must keep in mind that we ask our students to embrace that uncomfortable sensation and the onslaught of steep learning curves we offer them. If we want our students to open themselves up to new learning and risk being vulnerable, we must drive fear and sarcasm out of our classrooms and schools.

There are countless teachers like Sam Lewiston who believe that fear inspires higher achievement. His values are reflected in the comment he made to me: "If I were to adopt a different approach, I might find my classes to be more enjoyable, but I would sacrifice the satisfaction I get every day knowing that I am helping my students experience academic success." Sam and others like him will change only when they discover that their strategies make it more difficult to attain their worthy goal. Arguing with Sam would be futile. Because we share the same objective (high academic achievement by students), it is essential to develop a positive relationship with Sam and identify a commonality of purpose. Because Sam describes himself as "goal focused," showing him that there is a more effective way to achieve his goals than using his current methods will allow him to examine the true impact of the fear he engenders in his students. With effort, Sam can abandon his current practices and create a classroom that minimizes fear and supports the high achievement he wants for his students.

Getting Started

- Examine the language you use with students. "If you don't do well on the upcoming test, you are in danger of failing" can be switched to "By doing well on the upcoming test, you can earn a better grade." Both statements are true, but one deflates students by utilizing the language of fear, while the second statement encourages students by emphasizing the possibility of a positive outcome.

- Rather than cultivating an environment of fear, build a culture of success. Adopt the following three key messages, articulated by Saphier and Gower:

  This is important.

  You can do it.

  I won't give up on you. (1997, p. 296)

- Student behavior and performance mirror our expectations. Messages that induce fear communicate to students that we expect them to do poorly. "You can do it" and "I won't give up on you" communicate our belief that students will succeed.

- Many of our fear-driven practices are so habitual that we are unaware of them. Make it a practice to observe and be observed by a trusted colleague. Look for instances in which you unintentionally engage in behavior that creates fear in the learning environment. Together, you can discuss ways to change these destructive practices by replacing them with more positive messages that support learning.

- Don't confuse fear with a healthy respect for authority. It's crucial that students respect you and your authority, but they don't need to be afraid of you.

- Put yourself in your students' shoes by regularly learning new things. Learn to play a musical instrument. Study a foreign language. Intentionally put yourself in a situation where you are less skilled and you must meet externally imposed standards. When teachers find themselves being judged by others under circumstances in which they feel less than fully competent, they can better appreciate how vulnerable we feel when asked to learn something new and how destructive fear is to the learning process.

- Above all, remember that all new learning requires that students become vulnerable and take a risk as they move out of their comfort zones. When students are afraid, they focus on self-preservation rather than the acquisition of new knowledge and the development of new skills. By removing fear from the classroom, you encourage your students to take risks and learn more.

Minimize Your Use of Coercion

Human beings are driven to be autonomous and self-determining. We naturally resist when others attempt to exert undue control over us. By their very nature, however, schools are coercive organizations. The schedule is rigidly defined, from the length of class periods to the length of the school year. Students are told what they must study and what skills they must master from the time they begin kindergarten. In such an environment, coercion is rampant.

Their natural drive to be autonomous leads students to resist coercion. As you will see in this chapter, teachers who rely on coercion may have classrooms with few disruptions, but students will also have little interest in doing high-quality work. The only effective antidote is to provide as many choices as possible while working within a highly defined structure.

Ms. Lugo

The poster above the whiteboard in the front of the room unambiguously set the tone for Miranda Lugo's 7th grade English class. At the top, large type proclaimed: "Welcome to *My* World—Ms. Lugo." Smaller type below read: "Feel free to do what you'd like on your own time. I demand your compliance only during our time together."

Miranda Lugo has almost no discipline problems. She is as organized as any teacher I've ever observed. She is the epitome of "clear expectations." As students entered her classroom at the beginning of my observation, she greeted them warmly and reminded them, "You should have your independent reading book with you as well as your notebook. If you don't have it, quickly return to your locker so you will be well prepared and ready for a successful day." A few students scurried to their lockers with a minimum of disruption.

As students prepared to work quietly on the "problem of the day," Ms. Lugo told them, "Please place your 250- to 300-word 'compare and contrast' paper on the upper left-hand corner of your desk so I can collect it while you complete the problem of the day. Thank you. As you know, if your paper is late or does not conform to the posted guidelines, I will be calling your home."

Before beginning her formal instruction, Ms. Lugo asked if there were any questions about the upcoming report. Students were studying the American Civil War in social studies, and Ms. Lugo had asked each student to research a person from this conflict as part of the English class. Each student needed to report on a different person.

"I have a question," said Colin. "I wanted to do my paper on Lincoln, but Antoine already picked him, so you said I couldn't do Lincoln."

"That's right," replied Ms. Lugo. "What's the question?"

"Why can't Lincoln be written about by more than one student?"

"I'm trying to ensure that you have a wide perspective," answered Ms. Lugo. "Lincoln is certainly worthy of study. But there are many other men and women who played an important role in the Civil War. I'm sure you'll find someone else interesting."

"But," Colin protested, "what difference does it make if two of us write about Lincoln or Jefferson Davis or whoever?"

In an even tone, Ms. Lugo simply stated, "Colin, you see the poster every day when you walk in. This is *my* classroom. I will ask you just one question: Is what I am telling you to do in any way unfair?"

"No, it's not unfair," admitted Colin. "It just seems stupid."

"It may seem stupid to you," answered Ms. Lugo without a hint of anger or upset. "But I need you to comply with what you have correctly identified as a fair expectation. OK?"

"Yeah, sure," replied Colin. "Whatever."

"Ms. Lugo, I have a question," said Aaron. "What happens if Colin does his paper on Lincoln even though Antoine already picked him?"

"Aaron, you know the answer to that question. I approve your selections for all writing assignments and projects. If anyone were to choose to do something without my approval, they would receive no credit. It's explained in the 'Class Rules and Expectations' sheet I distributed and reviewed with you the first day of school. I know none of you want to fail, and it certainly seems foolish to do all that work for no credit. Any other questions?"

There were none.

Students were given the final 10 minutes of class to read silently from their independent reading book. As class was about to end, Ms. Lugo asked students to look to the front of the room, where she had posted the homework. "The only thing you need to do this evening is to write five to seven lines in your journals reflecting on the reading you have done today, plus read an additional 20 minutes this evening. Remember that journal entries are to be done in black or blue ink." As the bell rang, Ms. Lugo smiled and said, "That's it. Have a great day. I look forward to seeing you tomorrow."

The Students' Perspective

Later that day, I spoke with Colin and Aaron about Ms. Lugo's class and style. I chose these two students because they had questioned Ms. Lugo about her rule that only one student could report on any given figure from the Civil War.

"From your comments in class, Colin, I take it that you don't especially like or appreciate Ms. Lugo's guidelines regarding the project," I began.

"It's like I said," replied Colin. "It just seems stupid. It's not that big a deal. She just has all these rules, and things always have to be done her way. I mean, I don't know why she can't just lighten up a bit and let us do what we want." The more Colin talked, the more agitated he appeared.

"So will you do the paper and follow her guidelines, even if you think it's foolish?" I asked.

"Of course," answered Colin. "I'm not stupid. I'll just do it and get it done. I'll pick some lame name from our list and give her what she wants. It's easier than fighting and losing."

"I'm curious, Colin. Do you think you'll enjoy the project at all? Will you do your best work?"

"Are you serious?" Colin asked with a laugh. "I'll do the project, but 'enjoy it'? You've got to be joking. I'll give Ms. Lugo what she demands because I don't need the headache of fighting a control freak, but the idea of 'enjoying it' and 'doing my best work' is pretty absurd."

"What about you, Aaron? You asked the question about what would happen if Colin didn't follow the rules."

"Oh, I was just playing around and killing a little class time," Aaron answered. "I knew what Ms. Lugo was going to say. I just think it's funny to hear her get off on all her rules and regulations like it's such a big deal."

"Will you do the project and follow the guidelines?" I asked.

"Most definitely. See, Ms. Lugo has everything figured out in terms of points and value. This Civil War project counts a lot. It would be dumb not to give her what she wants in this case. But other times I blow things off and take the zero, if it's not worth that many points or whatever. You just have to make sure you do it with stuff that won't end up causing you to fail."

"Wait a second," I said, dumbfounded by what I was hearing. "Are you saying you sometimes intentionally ignore assignments or purposefully do them incorrectly even though you know you'll get no credit?"

"Absolutely," answered Aaron with an impish grin. "Blowing off an assignment is pretty fun, but the most cool thing is to do the assignment in a way where you know Ms. Lugo can't give you credit because it violates some stupid rule."

"How is that fun? And don't you care about your grade?" I was amazed and intrigued by what Aaron was telling me.

"It's fun because I just like doing what I want to do and I know it drives her crazy! From the time I get up until I go to bed every day,

I have people telling me what I 'have to' do. When I can do what I want without risking failure, that's pretty awesome. Plus, I know it confuses Ms. Lugo, and it's always fun to watch someone who has all the answers be confused!"

"And the lower grade doesn't bother you?"

"Like I said, I'd never do it if it meant failing the class. I don't feel like going to summer school or repeating the year. But to tell you the truth, it doesn't really matter if I get an *A* or a *D*. I know Ms. Lugo and most other teachers take this stuff way serious, but this is 7th grade! It's not like it's going to change my future if I do really great or do really lousy. It's not as important as you adults like to pretend it is."

"Would you say your attitude is typical, or are you an exception?" I asked.

"I think I might be a little extreme. Most kids don't go so far as blowing off assignments. But I know that most kids don't like being told what to do and exactly how to do it all the time. It gets old pretty fast. My guess is that most kids do just enough to get through and don't think about it much."

"One last question," I said. "Do you think Ms. Lugo inspires any kids to study English in the future?"

The two boys looked at each other and started laughing. "Not really," said Colin. "It's, like, impossible to be inspired when someone's telling you what to do all the time."

"Seriously," added Aaron. "She's the boss and we'll do what we need to in order to get by, but that's as far as it goes."

Ms. Lugo's Teaching Philosophy

"I'm sure the boys regaled you with stories about how coercive I am and how I have too many rules and regulations," Miranda Lugo began. "I assure you, I'm not the ogre they sometimes make me out to be."

"Please," I assured her, "the boys did not paint you as an ogre. Of course, they grumbled about your strict guidelines, but I'd like to have you tell me why you structure your class the way you do."

"Certainly. These are middle school kids, and they need a lot of structure. In fact, the more structure and the less wiggle room you give them, the more successful they'll be.

"I pride myself on being highly organized. Organization is probably the biggest single hurdle for middle school kids. Most of them have the intelligence to be successful, but elementary school doesn't require tremendous organizational skills. In middle school, they encounter multiple teachers, different styles, and different approaches. It can be overwhelming. Those teachers who allow too much freedom for middle school kids feed into their penchant for disorganization."

"What's your approach?" I asked.

"Structure and organization. I tell the kids on day 1 what my requirements are. I tell them that what I demand from them is non-negotiable, but that if they do what I require, they are guaranteed to be successful. To build them up, I tell them that I know in my heart each one of them wants to be successful and that all they need to do is follow my instructions explicitly and they will achieve their goals. In short, I offer them a surefire recipe for academic success in a challenging environment."

"Middle school kids can be a challenge. Do they accept what you tell them?"

"For the most part, yes. There will always be the rare kid who comes from an unsupportive environment or who has emotional issues that negatively impact his or her performance, but on the whole, my students comply with my requirements. I think administration knows that a higher percentage of my students complete their homework, turn in papers and projects on time, and complete course requirements. I don't mean to be simplistic, but it really boils down to structure, organization, and being clear about expectations."

"Can you tell me about the quality of the work you receive from your students?" I asked.

"In our middle school, like most middle schools, we operate with a team concept. Each of the teams has a cross section of the population. Therefore, the quality of the work I receive runs clear across the bell curve. I have my high-achieving students and my low-achieving students. Most fall somewhere in the middle."

"I ask because I'm interested in whether your students simply do *more* work or if they do *higher-quality* work," I continued.

"I know my students do *more* work. I'd like to believe that they do higher-quality work as well, but I'm not sure about that. Regardless, even if my only victory is getting students to do more work, I feel comfortable with that. I'm helping them develop a sense of responsibility. Too many kids today lack the sense of responsibility needed to be successful as adults. Providing kids with a kind but firm set of nonnegotiables prepares them to succeed in the world of work."

"Is there anything else you'd like to add?" I asked.

"Yes," said Miranda. "As you can probably tell, I take my job very seriously. It's my responsibility to motivate my students and make sure they complete all of their assignments. Too many teachers provide kids with choice because they naively believe that students will make wise decisions on their own. I see myself as a caring, nurturing teacher, but it's foolish to think that middle school kids will work hard and make good decisions if we don't force them to work hard. I've learned over the years that students only work as hard as we make them work. While there may be a few internally motivated students, the vast majority will do as little as possible. It's my responsibility to make them do as much work as possible. Anything less compromises the education our students deserve."

Commentary

The limit of coercion is compliance. Most of Miranda Lugo's students complete their work, but by her own admission, there is no evidence that they produce higher-quality work or learn more than their peers. My conversation with two of Miranda's students illustrates two common ways students act in a coercive situation. Colin is the "typical" student, in that he will comply but never be inspired. School and learning certainly aren't enjoyable for kids like Colin. Teachers who hope to inspire their students need them to become excited about learning. Students who are regularly coerced generally will do what is necessary but will never do more.

Aaron is less typical, but his story is nonetheless interesting. The Aarons of our classrooms show us that some kids are so driven by their need to be autonomous that they will even sacrifice good grades in order to be self-determining. While Aaron identified himself as savvy enough to determine which assignments he could skip, some students are so driven to be autonomous that they will even accept failure (and its attendant consequences) to retain control of their lives.

It is interesting to note that both Colin and Aaron characterize Mrs. Lugo's strict adherence to rules as "not a big deal." Their behavior suggests that it is, indeed, a very big deal to both boys. Colin grew noticeably agitated as he talked about a coercive situation he saw as "stupid." Aaron's willingness to take a lower grade in order to establish his autonomy offers compelling evidence that the lack of freedom these students feel is very important to him. Adolescents commonly engage in the strategy of denial, especially when they feel powerless. When students tell you it's "no big deal" or answer with a terse "whatever" when you ask a question, it is always wise to attend to their behavior rather than their words. To save face, students will often claim that things are not problematic, even as their actions tell a very different story.

Many teachers like Miranda erroneously believe that students aren't motivated. They are mistaken. Like all of us, students are internally motivated, but not necessarily in the way we would like them to be. During my observation of Miranda's class, Aaron was motivated to "kill a little class time" by questioning his teacher. At times, his motivation to prove he is in charge of his own life manifests in his refusal to do assignments he believes are not that important. At other times, he is motivated to earn the passing grade that keeps him from having to attend summer school or repeat the course, so he complies with his teacher's requirements. These are all instances of internal motivation—but not the kind Miranda is looking for.

Great teachers inspire students to be motivated to learn and perform to the best of their ability. Among other things, that requires a strong relationship, which I will discuss in Chapter 7. Teachers will not succeed in inspiring their students by relying on coercion, as Miranda Lugo does. There is enough coercion in school already, including mandatory attendance, a minimum number of school days, a minimum number of hours of attendance, course requirements for graduation, and an increasing number of high-stakes tests that must be passed in order to be promoted or graduate. Coercion is the enemy of quality. Inspirational teachers eliminate all unnecessary coercion in an effort to encourage academic achievement and a love of learning in their students.

Getting Started

- Because coercion will always be a part of the educational landscape, balance it with as much choice as possible. Choice in the classroom can be as simple as giving your students the option of doing two equally valid assignments. Remember that every choice you offer acts as a counterweight to the requirements and nonnegotiables that exist in every classroom.
- There is a fine line between being structured and organized and being coercive. Effective teachers are organized and provide sufficient structure for their students to be successful in an environment that minimizes coercion and allows for student choice.
- Give your students as much freedom as they can responsibly manage. Be honest with your students, telling them that you will give them as many choices and as much freedom as you can while maintaining the educational integrity of the classroom. Let them know that there will be times when there will be no options provided and you will ask them to do it "your way." Students who have sufficient freedom and choice rarely grumble when they are occasionally unavailable.
- Engage students when developing class rules and routines. Giving them a sense of control over this part of their school day will result in fewer discipline problems and greater acceptance of the rules you develop.
- Provide as much choice as you can without sacrificing your authority or the educational objective of your lesson. In one

school I know, students can create their own alternative to any assignment *as long as the alternative they create addresses the same educational objective as the assignment created by the teacher.* The teachers in this school report to me that the vast majority of students complete the teacher-created assignments. The simple fact that the students have an option removes the coercion from the situation. Those few divergent thinkers who create alternative assignments simply help teachers expand their repertoires for subsequent classes.

- Be certain that your students are conscious of the choices you offer. When students perceive the classroom as providing adequate freedom, it immediately feels less coercive. The result will be fewer power struggles and more on-task behavior.

Eliminate External Rewards

Providing external rewards for learning is such a widely used practice that it borders on heresy to even question this time-honored tradition. The belief in the efficacy of external rewards is so pervasive that some schools even offer students monetary incentives for good grades.

Regardless of their intent, external rewards unintentionally communicate that learning and the acquisition of academic competence are not inherently valuable. Behind the smiles, words of encouragement, and tangible rewards provided to compliant students lurks an unsettling truth: the bestowing of external rewards interferes with the natural desire to learn and develop competence. In this chapter, you will see how the systematic use of external rewards for academic achievement sabotages our ability to inspire students to develop a love of learning.

Ms. Jaegger

Beth Jaegger's 4th grade students were practically bursting with excitement as they entered the classroom Thursday morning.

"Check it out!" squealed Carrie, running to examine the wall hanging that showed how close the students were to earning another movie. "If everyone did their homework last night, we'll be over the top and get to see another movie tomorrow! This is awesome!" Other students joined Carrie and traded high fives in anticipation of hearing the good news from their teacher.

"Good morning, boys and girls," said Ms. Jaegger. "I am pretty sure by the look on your faces that everyone decided to complete your homework last night. Am I right?"

"Yes!" the students nearly screamed in chorus.

"Awesome!" said Ms. Jaegger. "And what does that mean?" she asked, knowing the answer but wanting the excitement to build and linger for a moment longer.

"Movie time!" the class cheered.

"That's right. And some of you have earned a homework pass as well. That might come in handy when we have a particularly challenging assignment and you just don't feel like doing any work.

"You know what?" Ms. Jaegger continued. "I'm so pleased with how well you guys are doing that I'm going to give you a chance to earn a special treat. We have a difficult math lesson coming up today." The smiles almost immediately disappeared and were replaced by several groans. "Hey, no complaining. Like it or not, we have to work, but I think you'll like what I'm going to offer you. If you give me your full attention during the math lesson—and I'll tell you right now it won't be particularly exciting—*and* if everyone completes the worksheet I'm going to give you and brings it to class tomorrow morning, we'll add popcorn to our Friday afternoon movie party!"

The excitement that had disappeared with the mention of work returned full bore with the offer of popcorn.

"OK, guys. Looks like we have a deal. Now, no complaining. We can't have fun all the time. This is school, remember, not playtime. I'm sure we can get through this together and give ourselves an early start to the weekend."

With a minimum of fuss, the students took out their math text and followed along as Ms. Jaegger taught the math lesson. On a couple of occasions when a student showed signs of losing focus, the teacher would make a comment like, "I can almost smell that buttery popcorn now!" or "It would be a shame to watch a movie without scrumptious popcorn just because one or two people choose not to behave." With these gentle prompts from Ms. Jaegger and a few peer comments ("C'mon, Marcus. Don't ruin it for everyone." "Hey, Yvonne, just be quiet. We're almost done."), the students managed to complete the lesson to the teacher's satisfaction. In fact, because they had done what she asked, she announced, "I'm giving you guys 10 minutes of free time before we go to lunch. You may read a book, draw, or talk quietly with a friend. Just remember to keep the noise down because the students in Ms. Voight's room are still working, poor things."

The Students' Perspective

I had made arrangements with Beth to speak with Carrie and Marcus. "Is it OK with them to spend their lunchtime with me?" I asked.

"No problem," answered Beth. "I figured they would be a good pair for you to chat with. Gives you the whole spectrum with just two kids. As soon as I told Marcus I'd give him an extra homework pass, he was all for it! And Carrie is always looking for ways to accumulate extra points, so she volunteered right away. I figured she'd be a good kid to talk to since she does so well with rewards."

"So Carrie earns points for talking with me?" I asked. I didn't admit it to Beth, but I felt slightly less legitimate, knowing that the students were being "paid" to speak with me.

"Absolutely," said Beth. "I run just about everything on a token economy. Regardless of what students are doing, they always earn or lose points. I want them to be prepared for what it's like in the real world. Oh, here they are now. Have a great conversation!" Beth Jaegger slipped out of the room and left me with two smiling 4th grade students.

"Seems like you guys enjoy your class and teacher. Am I right?" I began.

"Yes," they answered, heads nodding vigorously.

"I'm interested in what you like most about your class," I continued.

"The movies," said Marcus, a huge smile spreading across his face. "I got me some friends in other classes, and tomorrow afternoon they'll be slaving away doing all kinds of work while we'll be chilling out watching a movie and eating us some popcorn."

"You enjoy anything else?" I asked.

"Well," said Marcus, "I like field trips, but them are hard to get. Sometimes it seems like Ms. Jaegger is just saying stuff about a trip to the museum or to a beach or whatnot, but it's just a way to trick us into doing more work. Seems like most times, we don't quite get there. But the movies is pretty easy to get, so that's cool."

I turned to Carrie. "What about you? You sure seemed excited when you walked into class this morning. I'm guessing you like the movies as well."

"I do," Carrie agreed. "Tomorrow will be real fun. Like Marcus said, it's way better than doing boring work. But I really just like earning as many points as I can earn. I don't know if Ms. Jaegger told you, but I have the most points of anyone in class. I have enough homework passes to last me a month!"

"Hey, you want to slide a couple of those my way?" Marcus ventured.

"Marcus, don't be ridiculous," Carrie answered. "First of all, the homework passes have our names on them, so mine wouldn't even help you. You'd know that if you got more."

"Let me switch the topic for a minute," I said. "Tell me your favorite subject."

"That's easy," said Carrie. "Math."

"Why?" I asked. "Are you good in math?"

"I don't really know if I'm good at it. I just like it because you can get more points in math than anything else. Like, it's harder to earn points in language arts. And Ms. Jaegger doesn't give points for things like art and music or gym. But you can earn a lot of points in math if you just be quiet and do your work."

"What about you, Marcus?"

"Me? I like gym mostly. I mean, you don't get no points or nothing, but I like it because I get to move around and I'm good at it and it's fun. The regular classes are OK, I guess. I try to be good and not mess up so the class can get our movies and such. Carrie, she's always trying to get points. I'm just trying not to lose any or mess up too much. But Ms. Jaegger, she's cool. Like today when she kind of reminded me to chill so we could have that sweet popcorn tomorrow. That will be nice. Indeed."

"Carrie," I said, "I'm curious. If Ms. Jaegger didn't award points, do you think math would still be your favorite subject?"

A look of panic crossed Carrie's face. "Oh, my God," she gasped. "Did Ms. Jaegger tell you she was going to stop giving points? Is that why she asked you to talk to us?"

"No, not at all," I assured her.

"You had me frightened!" she said with a laugh. "What was your question again?"

"I asked if math would still be your favorite if there were no points to be earned."

Carrie seemed genuinely puzzled by the question and remained silent for a few moments. "I'm not really sure," she said tentatively. "I mean, I do my work now so I can earn points, and I like math because I can earn a lot, but I never really thought about *liking* math, if you know what I mean." I did. "I'm not trying to be mean or anything," she continued, "but I think your question is kind of confusing. I'm glad you said Ms. Jaegger is not going to stop giving us points. It makes everything so much easier and gives us a reason to work hard and learn. Otherwise, what's the point?"

What a great question!

Ms. Jaegger's Teaching Philosophy

"Did Carrie and Marcus behave well?" Beth Jaegger asked as we sat down for our conversation.

"They were fine. Great kids," I answered.

"Good," she said. "I think I'll give them each an extra homework pass for being so cooperative. A little extra reward when they're not expecting it is really effective. And goodness knows, Marcus can use that homework pass," Beth added with a laugh. "Although I don't know what Carrie will do with hers. She must have enough to paper her room. She just loves to earn those rewards. I'll bet she made sure to tell you that."

"She sure did," I said. "In fact, she identified math as her favorite subject because she has the opportunity to earn the most points."

"That's interesting," Beth said. "Carrie's a model student and is very compliant. She really is the perfect student for any reward or incentive program. Still, I'm surprised that she identified math as her favorite subject. She seems to enjoy reading and writing more, and she certainly has more talent in the language arts area." Beth paused before adding, "I guess that pretty much sums up the power of positive reinforcement, doesn't it? To think, something so simple can have such a profound impact on a student's attitude toward a subject."

"Do you think she'd maintain such a positive attitude if you were to offer fewer incentives?" I asked.

"I'm not sure," admitted Beth, "but it's a moot point. It would be foolish to abandon something that works so well, not just for Carrie but for all of my students."

"Have you always used incentive programs with your students?" I asked.

"It was certainly something emphasized in our teacher prep courses," answered Beth. "We spent a lot of time discussing fixed and intermittent schedules of reinforcement and punishment. I never liked the punishment part of behavior management. I think it's really important for kids to like school, so I try to avoid punishment as much as possible. I might need to remind kids that there could be an unpleasant consequence, but I like to give them a warning before they are in real danger of losing the reward they are working for. Like in class today—I had to speak to both Marcus and Yvonne, but by using some positive peer pressure and reminding them of the movie and popcorn, I was able to shape their behavior pretty effectively, I think."

"I certainly agree that the kids seem to enjoy earning both individual and group rewards. My concern is that the kids seem focused on earning points and incentives and give very little attention to learning."

"Being focused on earning incentives gets them to do work— some of it quite tedious, I might add. I admit that I sometimes 'trick' them into working hard, but I don't apologize for making kids work and succeed. Without a well-structured incentive program, most kids simply wouldn't work. They are no different from us. We get paid to work; that's our reward. I can't pay my students, but I certainly can let them watch a movie, earn some free time, and give them a homework pass so they can take a night off when they don't feel like dealing with an especially difficult or uninspiring homework assignment. Wouldn't you agree that my students are motivated?" asked Beth.

"From what I observed, I'm sure your students are highly motivated—at least to watch a movie, have popcorn, and earn a homework pass," I replied.

Commentary

There is no doubt that Beth Jaegger wants only the best for her students. That she is a kind, caring person is illustrated by her reluctance to use punishment, the other side of the coin in the reward/punishment model. Beth's classroom, her students' comments, and her own words illustrate the "problem" with providing external rewards for academic achievement.

"Do rewards motivate people? Absolutely. They motivate people to get rewards" (Kohn, 1993, p. 67). As Alfie Kohn points out in *Punished by Rewards*, rewards work—and that's the problem. My observation of Beth's classroom and her students clearly showed a group of kids who are highly motivated. And what, exactly, did Beth's students want? They wanted to watch a movie. They wanted to eat popcorn. They wanted to earn a homework pass. There was not a single mention by Beth Jaegger or her students about the value of learning or academics. In fact, even as Beth attempted to motivate her students with the incentive of popcorn and a movie, she introduced the upcoming math lesson by saying, "It won't be particularly exciting." She later cautioned the class, "We can't have fun all the time. This is school, remember, not playtime. I'm sure we can get through this together and give ourselves an early start to the weekend."

I have no doubt that Beth values education and learning. What makes the use of external rewards for learning so insidious is that when we provide external, tangible rewards to students, we inadvertently devalue education and learning. The unintentional but powerful message we provide to students is this: "What we are asking you to learn is not worth learning in its own right. What we are asking you to do is not inherently valuable. It is worth the effort only because if you do what we ask, you will get something valuable, like watching a movie, having some popcorn, or talking quietly with a classmate."

Virtually all teachers offer rewards and incentives in their classrooms. Every teacher preparation program I know of provides direct instruction on how to "shape" student behavior through the systematic presentation of rewards. The reward approach to education and classroom management is so prevalent in education today that to challenge it is almost unheard of.

But educators have an obligation to scrutinize all practices and examine their true impact. Carrie's and Marcus's comments reveal the unintended consequence of a well-developed reward program. "Model student" Carrie enjoys math because she can easily earn a lot of points and agrees with Marcus that watching a movie is preferable to "boring work." There is no evidence of Carrie being excited about learning and developing new competencies. Is it any wonder? She never experiences the thrill of learning on its own. Instead, she is systematically bombarded with the message that the goal is to accumulate as many points as possible.

What about Marcus? He expresses an affinity for physical education class because he gets to move and demonstrate competence. It's his favorite part of the school day, even though he doesn't earn any points. What he gets is an experience that matches his learning style and an opportunity to succeed. As for his regular academic classes, Marcus would be delighted to simply score another homework pass so he can avoid as much work as possible.

Even though many students comply with the teacher's demands in order to earn rewards, there are students who seem impervious to the seductive power of whatever incentives the teacher has to offer. Why? These students are highly driven by the need for freedom and would rather assert their autonomy than earn a reward and feel manipulated. In Chapter 2, we met Aaron, a student who admitted that sometimes he intentionally misses assignments because he knows he will still pass his class. He is willing to get a lower grade because defying his teacher helps him assert control over his life. The same process is at play with students who are capable of easily earning incentives but routinely choose not to. When we consider the universal drive toward self-governance, their noncompliance makes perfect sense.

Notice that I have decried the use of *external* rewards for learning, not the cultivation of *internal* rewards. Every time we learn something new, master some difficult concept, or increase our level of competence, we are internally rewarded. When we achieve success, our brains release endorphins, powerful chemicals that make us feel good. The natural reward for learning is the good feeling we experience when we accomplish something. Paradoxically, working for external rewards diminishes the power of the internal reward system already wired into us. When we externally reward students in the classroom, we devalue learning and interfere with the body's natural mechanism for rewarding learning and achievement.

There is nothing easier than gently reworking your current incentive system to be more effective. All you need to do is exchange your reward system for recognition and affirmation. Let me explain.

The wall hanging that Carrie excitedly examined at the beginning of the chapter does not have to be tied to an external reward. Students thrive on feedback, and letting them know how close they are to achieving individual or group goals is helpful. Because students are naturally driven to achieve, it is helpful for them to see their progress. Keep the charts and posters, but let the excitement of achievement be the reward, rather than contaminating the joy of learning with a movie, pizza party, or, even worse, a homework pass (a clear signal that the objective of hard work is to avoid work and learning). When you recognize and celebrate learning for its own sake rather than providing external rewards, you will support your students' natural desire to learn.

There is a monumental difference between rewarding and affirming. Rewarding is externally imposed and unintentionally implies that hard work and learning are not valuable in and of themselves.

Affirmation is a very different, powerful way to support the drive to achieve. The next time a student does something well, resist the temptation to externally reward him or her, even with something so apparently benign as verbal praise. Instead, ask the student how he or she feels and what it is like to have experienced success. In that moment, the student will discover a powerful truth: *working hard and learning feel good.* After the student has had a chance to consciously experience how good it feels to be successful (even if it's just for a moment), provide affirmation by saying something like, "You have every reason to be happy and feel proud of yourself. Congratulations. I'm happy for you!"

By affirming rather than rewarding, we are helping our students discover that learning feels good and that we are there to celebrate with them. Let them *own* the experience first. Then ensure that they make the connection and support them in their natural desire to become increasingly competent.

Getting Started

- Immediately give up as many external rewards for learning as possible.
- Move from rewarding to affirming. Have students identify the positive feelings they experience when they are successful. The natural desire to learn will be strengthened when students realize how good they feel when they succeed. Once students identify that achievement feels good, affirm their success. Never dilute this powerful discovery with the presentation of a tangible external reward.
- Talk with students about the kind of learners they want to be. When they discover that they want to be successful students who work hard, learning will become its own reward.
- Distinguish between *rewards* and *celebrations.* I supervised teachers who created a reward program that required students to read a certain number of pages in two weeks in order to earn the right to watch a movie. The students grudgingly complied, but reading was reduced to a "hoop" that needed to

be jumped through. With my encouragement, the following year the teachers abandoned the reward program. They told the students they were going to chart how much reading they completed during a two-week period because they were curious how much the students read. At the conclusion of the two weeks, the students watched a movie, but it was not something they "earned" based on how much reading they had done. The results? Students read as much the second year and made more positive comments about the reading they had completed instead of complaining that they "had to read." Maintain your celebrations, but give up reward programs that diminish the joy and value of learning.

- If you insist on giving rewards to your students, don't give things like a "homework pass," which communicates to them that it is desirable to avoid working hard and learning.

Discover the Power
of Internal Motivation

The vast majority of schools and classrooms rely on the reward/ punishment model. Make no mistake: this model works very well for some students. Students who come from supportive homes and who value learning often fare quite well. The problem is that the reward/punishment approach doesn't work well enough for the majority of students. Too many are left behind, failing to reach their potential. This way of understanding human behavior and motivation has taken us as far as it can. We need to reexamine what motivates our students so that we can more effectively educate tomorrow's citizenry.

This chapter will introduce the concept of internal control psychology, a completely different approach to motivation. Teachers have a responsibility to bring out the best in their students. To do so, they need to have a thorough grasp of what drives human behavior. Well acquainted with a sound theory and equipped with the knowledge that humans are internally motivated, we can create schools and classrooms in which significantly more students are inspired to engage in high-quality work and put forth the effort needed for academic excellence. If we are serious about educational improvement, it's time to embrace a new way to educate—one based on the principles of internal control psychology.

The Theory of Internal Control Psychology

Chapters 1, 2, and 3 of this book introduced the cornerstones of the external control model of human motivation:

- Fear: "If you don't do what we tell you, you'll be sorry."
- Coercion: "We can make you behave the way you should, and it's our responsibility to motivate you."
- Reward/Reinforcement: "We'll make learning worthwhile by giving you something you want."

I propose that educators move to a completely different model for understanding human motivation. We are not controlled from the outside, as the reward/punishment model would have us believe. On the contrary, we are internally motivated. We constantly behave in ways that we believe will make the world reflect what we want at that moment.

There are various permutations of internal control psychology. I practice and teach choice theory, developed by William Glasser, M.D. This chapter provides a synopsis of some major components of choice theory; the following chapters illustrate how to implement the concepts of internal control psychology in your classroom and school.

Many educators pride themselves on being pragmatic practitioners who have little time for or interest in theory. More action-oriented, they prefer strategies they can immediately apply in the classroom. "Why waste precious time on theory?" they wonder. It's a fair question and one that I would like to answer.

Successful teaching—and indeed, success in any undertaking based on human interaction—requires a thorough understanding of motivation and behavior. Most of us have been raised and educated with the external control model of reward and punishment. While a model based upon fear, coercion, and external rewards can be effective to a point, it cannot inspire large numbers of students to do high-quality work. To improve our schools in any appreciable way, we need to implement the internal control psychology that more accurately explains human behavior. As long as we are only knowledgeable about the flawed psychology of external control, we will never be able to substantially improve our interactions with others and be more successful as educators. Once we are well versed in internal control psychology, we can create schools, classrooms, and relationships that foster academic excellence in many more students.

I want to offer a theoretical overview to avoid the "cookbook" approach found in too many texts that do little more than provide exhaustive lists of classroom strategies. No matter how valid the strategies, there will be instances where you encounter a situation that will fall outside the scope of what has been described in even the most comprehensive book. In those cases, it's crucial to have a solid grasp of the psychology that best explains human behavior and motivation. With that in mind, let's examine some of the key aspects of internal control psychology.

Basic Needs

All behavior, from birth until death, is purposeful, engaged in so that we can meet five human drives:

- To survive and be safe and secure
- To connect and belong
- To achieve power and competence
- To be free and autonomous
- To play, enjoy, and have fun

Because these drives are common to all people, they are often called the basic needs. The needs represent the "nature" side of the coin in the nature/nurture mixture. The educational environment we create represents the "nurture" side of the coin and is at least as important as the nature side woven into our basic needs.

Most educators are familiar with Abraham Maslow's hierarchy of needs. In Maslow's model, individuals must meet lower-level needs like survival and safety before they can turn their attention to higher-order needs like self-esteem and self-actualization. The needs identified in choice theory do not exist as a pyramid or hierarchy. Just as there are people who are taller and people who are shorter, the strength of the basic needs differs from person to person. Like other things in nature, the strength of the basic needs falls along a normal distribution curve, with most people having need strength that is "typical." There are, however, people whose needs are especially strong or weak in a given area. My older daughter has an especially strong need to connect and belong. Both my son and I have a particularly strong need to be free and autonomous. My wife's need for safety and survival is stronger than that of anyone else in our immediate family.

The difference in need strength among our students highlights the importance of differentiated instruction. While our underlying educational objectives may be the same for all students, differentiated instruction allows us to create lesson plans with the need profiles of our students in mind so that more students can achieve academic excellence. Lessons ideally suited to one student may be less successful with others because of the strength of the basic needs each student brings to the classroom. The work of Carol Ann Tomlinson (1999, 2003; Tomlinson & McTighe, 2006) is particularly useful for teachers interested in creating a classroom where all students can achieve success through differentiated instruction.

Generally speaking, educators are most concerned with their students' need to achieve power and competence. We want to inspire our students so that their natural desire to achieve expresses itself in the pursuit of academic excellence. It is important to remember that although there is a natural drive to be powerful and competent, we do not instinctively know *how* to gain power and competence. In fact, many people develop power in destructive ways, such as by becoming bullies or using their influence to harm others.

The need for survival, safety, and security is especially evident when people "downshift" to survival. In these circumstances, the individual is so preoccupied with being safe that he or she has little emotional energy available to attend to other needs. When we introduce fear into the educational environment, the need for safety and survival dominates the attention of our students, and they are less driven by the need to develop academic competence. Chapter 1 offered a glimpse into a classroom saturated by fear. We saw students operating from a survival perspective; for example, Marcy, a successful student, indicated she would never say anything "controversial or risky" in Sam Lewiston's class because fear permeated the environment. The need for safety and survival dominating her consciousness in that class kept her from engaging in creative, risk-taking behaviors that fuel academic excellence.

Individuals with an especially high need for safety and survival tend to avoid taking risks. Those whose drive for safety and survival is less strong are more willing to take chances. At certain developmental stages, people tend to be more or less concerned with safety and survival because the strength of our needs ebbs and flows throughout the course of our lives. Adolescents, for example, are much more likely to be risk takers than younger children. Even within a given developmental period, however, we see individuals with particularly strong or relatively weak basic needs compared to their cohort. Just observe a typical school playground or physical education class for a few minutes, and you will likely see students with particularly high and low needs for safety and survival. Academic classrooms also reveal students across the spectrum. For example, students with a high need for safety and survival will only raise their hands when they are certain they have the correct answer. What we often refer to as "timidity" has its roots in the instinctive drive to be safe and secure.

The need to belong and connect is the social need we all share. The fact that need strength differs from person to person helps explain why social, cooperative learning activities are so successful with some students and so ineffective with others. Students with an especially strong need to connect will thrive academically when provided with a well-structured cooperative activity (although given a teacher with poor management skills and a group activity that is inadequately structured, these same students will waste academic time and be content to simply socialize). By the same token, if you put students with a low drive to connect into a cooperative group, they may flounder and possibly drag the group down, because the success of a cooperative group is determined in large measure by successful collaboration and interaction. While it is true that some students lack the specific skills to cooperate effectively with others, some simply lack the drive and have little inherent interest in social interaction.

Regardless of the strength of their need to connect, all students have *some* drive to belong and connect. Since students are driven by a social imperative, effective teachers structure their lessons so students can meet this need while engaging in rigorous academic work. Failure to offer students a chance to interact for long periods only invites off-task behavior that compromises learning.

We are all driven to make choices and exercise autonomy. In many ways, our humanity is defined by our ability to make choices. That fact that the desire for freedom is a fundamental human quality was powerfully described by psychiatrist Rollo May (1953) in *Man's Search for Himself*. May writes a parable of a man who is put in a cage and denied his freedom, all the while being very well taken care of and visited daily. Quickly the man becomes zombielike, his spirit destroyed by his lack of freedom. The need for freedom is especially important to address in schools, precisely because there are so many things that "must" be done and are nonnegotiable. Since school is somewhat coercive by its very nature, it is helpful to provide as many options to students as possible. Providing options does not mean that you "water down standards" or compromise the learning objectives. Instead, it means that you intentionally provide some choice and autonomy within a structure that supports your teaching objectives and the highest academic standards.

I have heard William Glasser emphasize the connection between fun and learning many times. My son helped me understand this concept many years ago.

"Hey, Dad," he said one evening, "look at this. Pretend you wanted to multiply 7/21 and 9/27. You can multiply 7 times 9. That's easy: 63. But 21 times 27 is pretty hard. But if you just reduce the fractions, you can make it 1/3 times 1/3. That's simple: 1/9."

"Who taught you that?" I asked.

"No one. I was just messing around and figured it out," Greg answered.

The next day, I asked Greg, "Was it fun when you figured out that fraction process?"

"Yeah, Dad," he answered enthusiastically. "It's always fun when you learn something new!" It was at that moment that I understood the strong link between fun and learning.

Walk into any great classroom, and the feeling of fun is palpable. It can be seen on the faces of the students. Just as importantly, it can be seen on the face and in the body language of the teacher. This doesn't mean that there is chaos and foolishness going on. On the contrary, the best classrooms are characterized by focused work in a joyful atmosphere. One of the best teachers I ever supervised as a school administrator often told parents, "We're all about the work in my classroom." This dedicated teacher was demanding and ran a highly structured, no-nonsense classroom. And I enjoyed visiting her room every day because it was a joyous, fun-filled room where active learning was on display regularly.

The external control model would have us believe that reactive students walk into our classes ready to be shaped by our presentation of rewards or punishments. In fact, students are internally driven by the needs built into their genetic code, and they behave in a never-ending quest to satisfy the universal needs to connect, be powerful, make choices, and have fun in a safe, secure environment. Our success as teachers is largely determined by how effective we are at creating learning environments where students can meet their needs by immersing themselves in the academic tasks we provide.

Wants and the Internal World

Whereas basic needs are universal and general drives, motivation is specific. I want to connect with *this person.* I feel competent and powerful when I engage in *this activity.* I am autonomous and have fun when doing *this activity.* As we experience enjoyment through need-satisfying experiences, we create a special collection of our most treasured people, behaviors, values, and beliefs. Choice theory refers to this concept as the quality world. I will refer to it as the *internal world,* the terminology I used in *Activating the Desire to Learn* (2007). While the label we use to identify this concept is not especially important, it is crucial to understand that the internal world is the source of all motivation. Whatever I place in my internal world is there because by being with that person or engaging in that behavior, I am able to satisfy the universal basic needs that constantly drive me.

For all intents and purposes, our internal world is empty at birth; we have not yet identified specific people, behaviors, values, or beliefs to motivate us in a specific way. Over time, as we interact with the world, we each build a unique internal world. As a family, school, and community, we have a profound impact on the creation of the internal world. How we raise and educate our children will help determine the kinds of belonging, power, freedom, fun, and survival pictures they put into their internal world.

Given poor guidance and little nurturing, a student may put gang membership into his or her internal world. Being in a gang can help an individual satisfy all of his or her needs. A less extreme but all too common example is one where a student puts bullying or disruption into his or her internal world. Those behaviors, as distasteful as they may be to us, can be addictively need-satisfying. If we want students to put school, learning, and working hard into their internal world, we must ensure that these activities are need-satisfying. If not, they will never be placed in the student's internal world and we will never see the kind of focused motivation and achievement we hope to see. The strategy I call "Plan with the Students' Needs in Mind" (see Chapter 10) will help you create lesson plans that are need-satisfying for your students.

Reality and Perception

Too many of us are quick to make comments like "He needs a dose of reality" or "She just doesn't get it" when another person simply perceives things differently than we do. How do we develop our perceptions? Three distinct filters contribute to our perception of reality: our sensory system, our current knowledge, and our values.

Reality exists outside us. To perceive external reality, we first need to access information on a sensory level. If we don't see it, hear it, feel it, taste it, or touch it, it does not exist for us. People with different sensory input will develop different perceptions, even if they were both in the same place.

Consider the following classroom example. You are a high school math teacher being formally observed by your department head. You are at the board, showing the class how to solve equations with multiple variables. Out of the corner of your eye, you see one of your students flicking paper at the student sitting in front of him. Knowing that physical proximity can be an effective management strategy, you leave the front of the room and position yourself near the offending student. You don't need to say a word, and the inappropriate behavior stops.

During your post-observation conference, the department head informs you that you would have been more effective had you remained at the front of the room as you discussed the process of solving equations. His "reality" was created without seeing the student flicking papers at a classmate. Even though we may share a common experience, each of us creates our own reality and behaves accordingly.

Situations like this abound. The role the sensory filter plays in the creation of perceptions explains why it is so important to arrange your classroom wisely. Ideally, you and every student would have maximum access to all essential sensory input while distractions were minimized. Strategically placing yourself as you teach and assist small groups and individuals minimizes the development of inaccurate perceptions due to incomplete sensory information. Additionally, you may have some students with identified sensory deficits that require special placement in the classroom.

Assuming information passes through our sensory filter without being compromised in any appreciable way, we next filter the incoming information against what we already know. Even though the external physical reality of the book in your hands at this very moment is identical for all readers, each reader perceives what is written here based on the preexisting knowledge he or she brings to the experience. Those well versed in internal control psychology perceive things differently from those who are unfamiliar with this explanation of human behavior, even though the printed words are the same for both readers.

The impact of the knowledge filter is felt in every classroom. I recently met a woman on an airplane who told me she had just completed a trip to Egypt with her grandson, who was in the 6th grade. In the school at which I last worked, our 6th grade students studied Egypt as part of the social studies curriculum. If that boy had been a student in our 6th grade, he would have perceived the unit about Egypt differently from most of his classmates because he had actually seen the pyramids, ridden on a camel, and experienced Egypt, even if only briefly.

Especially in the primary grades, the knowledge that students bring to the classroom varies widely and impacts their perceptions dramatically. Some have come from advantaged homes and have been to the zoo and museums or traveled to many places and seen people from various cultures speaking different languages. Others may have never traveled beyond a five-block radius from their home. As you teach (external reality), these students create perceptions based on the existing knowledge they have. Our educational system strives to provide common experiences to all students so the less advantaged children can "catch up" and develop the same rich perceptions as their more affluent peers.

Finally, all information from the outside world passes through our value filter, where we nonconsciously ascribe a positive, negative, or neutral value to an event. Our decision is always based upon what we want at that moment. Imagine a teacher who positively values active learning, cooperative group work, and student enthusiasm. As she scans her class, she sees close to 30 students clustered around the room in small groups, some of them sitting at tables, others standing. Although there is a fair amount of noise, she has a system that gets the students quiet and attentive in a matter of a few seconds. Sometimes students' voices get a little loud, but as she listens to what they are saying, she is delighted that the students are vigorously debating and discussing the topic she has asked them to explore. In addition to receiving the information on a sensory and knowledge level, she attaches a strong positive value to the experience because what she perceives closely matches what she wants at that moment.

Suddenly, she remembers that her supervisor is going to come to the room in just a couple of minutes for her annual formal evaluation! Imagine for a moment that this administrator believes that one essential quality of a good teacher is having the students silent most of the time, with occasional moments of conversation that rises barely above a whisper. Right or wrong, this administrator believes that kids are too boisterous by nature and need the structure of sitting in rows in a traditional classroom that is more teacher-centered than student-centered. She'll be there any moment.

This scenario illustrates an important point: internal world pictures are sometimes in conflict. The teacher values active learning. She is excited when the students get involved in a heated exchange about the topic they are studying. She is elated that the students are engaged and enthusiastic about learning. She also values her job and appreciates the importance of receiving a positive evaluation from the administrator. She knows that if she is observed at this moment, the administrator will not be pleased and her written evaluation will reflect her displeasure. The teacher's internal pictures are in conflict.

While there is no "right" way to resolve this conflict, let's assume that getting a favorable evaluation and keeping her job (professional survival) is more immediately compelling than demonstrating a teaching style that involves considerable student conversation, interaction, movement, and engagement. Because the desire to keep her job is so powerful, her perception of the class suddenly shifts and becomes decidedly negative. Even though "reality" hasn't changed at all in the intervening few seconds, she has shifted her perception from positive to negative once she remembers that her supervisor is about to observe her class. This does not mean that she values a positive evaluation *more than* she values creating a student-centered classroom. When internal pictures are in conflict—as they frequently are—we act based on what we want *at that moment*, not necessarily on what we believe is most important and representative of our deepest values and beliefs.

We talk about "reality" glibly, as if we all share the same reality. Because each of us has different sensory input, knowledge, and values, our perceptions of outside reality are often quite different from one another, and they can change instantaneously depending upon what we want at any given moment.

Internal Evaluation

At every moment, we compare our perception of reality and our picture of how we want things to be. Much of this comparing is out of awareness. When there is a match (or near match), we naturally continue to act in much the same way because our current behaviors are effective in helping us achieve our goals. When there is enough of a discrepancy, we change what we are doing so the world we perceive will more closely resemble the world we want. All behavior is purposeful because the intent of our behavior is to create a match between the perceived world and the internal world.

Let's return to the example of the teacher from the previous section. Initially, she perceived her class positively. Had her supervisor not been planning to observe the class, our teacher would have done everything possible to keep such a "great" class going so well. Because she was so pleased with how things were going, she would have maintained most of what she was doing, making only subtle changes that she thought would enhance an already positive teaching experience. With the realization that her supervisor was coming to observe the class and the knowledge that this administrator favors a traditional, teacher-centered classroom, our teacher immediately experienced the frustration we feel when we realize the world we perceive is very different from how we want it to be.

Since all behavior is purposeful, our teacher quickly gets the class in a more traditional classroom arrangement and informs the students they will do something different today because she is having a visitor who wants to observe her providing extended direct instruction to a well-behaved group of students. As the students conform to her requests, our teacher finds there is a match between how the class looks and what she wants at this moment. Notice that our teacher, like all of us, is motivated not by the outside world but by what she wants at that moment.

Some of you may point out that the teacher will likely resume her preferred approach once the formal observation is complete and her supervisor has left the room. I suspect you are right, because her internal pictures will also shift once her supervisor has left the room. She will once again be motivated to have the kind of classroom she had at the beginning of this scenario. This illustrates two important concepts:

- We have multiple internal world pictures, and they are often in conflict.
- We always act purposefully to get what we want *at that moment.*

This explains how students can *appear* sincere when they tell you they will complete their assigned homework and yet return to class the next day unprepared—again! While many of us falsely think the students were "playing us" or manipulating us, more often than not they were telling the truth at the time but didn't follow through because their pictures had changed in the interim.

While much of our internal evaluation occurs on a nonconscious level, it is wise to make our evaluations about education and academics conscious and intentional. This is the topic of Chapter 11.

Summary

We are born with powerful basic needs: to connect with others, to gain competence and power, to be autonomous, and to have fun and learn in a safe, secure environment. As we live our lives, we encounter people and engage in behaviors that help us satisfy these needs that drive us incessantly. We put need-satisfying people and behaviors, as well as values and beliefs, into our unique internal world, the source of all motivation. When students find school and learning to be a need-satisfying experience, they will put working hard and learning into their internal world and will be the academically motivated students we would like them to be.

Although we all live in the "real world," we each develop a perception of reality based on sensory input, current knowledge, and personal values. We then internally compare our perception of reality with the idealized picture we have in our internal world. We maintain or change our behavior in a purposeful attempt to create a match between what we perceive and what we want at that moment.

A superintendent in Dutchess County, New York, once said this after taking a four-day training session with me: "Choice theory reminds me of sailing. I can teach a person how to sail in about 30 minutes. They can then spend the next twenty years or more learning how to sail!" I have given you only the bare bones, but this outline provides you with enough information to start applying a new approach to understanding human behavior and motivation in your school and classroom. We can move beyond the limit of compliance offered by the carrot-and-stick model of external control psychology and intentionally create environments that will inspire more students to do higher-quality academic work. The following chapters examine specific strategies and applications of these concepts in the classroom and school.

Readers interested in a more comprehensive treatment of choice theory are encouraged to consult *Choice Theory* (Glasser, 1998) as well as *Activating the Desire to Learn* (Sullo, 2007) and *The Inspiring Teacher* (Sullo, 2008).

Getting Started

- Ask yourself if you believe in freedom and responsibility. (Remember that external control psychology denies freedom. Without freedom, there can be no responsibility.) Ask yourself if you believe in personal accountability. (Remember that external control psychology teaches that our behavior is fully determined by outside events and that our job is to "shape" the behavior of our students. If that's true, there can be no accountability.) If you come to the conclusion that you believe in freedom, responsibility, and personal accountability, then become familiar with internal control psychology and begin practicing it both personally and professionally.

- Begin by intentionally creating an environment where students can satisfy their needs by doing what you ask them to do. When you do this, you switch from trying to "motivate your students" to creating an environment where students will be internally motivated to do what you want them to do. This shift is as powerful as it is subtle and clarifies the lines of responsibility. Your job as a teacher is not to take responsibility for students' lives by "motivating them"; your job as a teacher is to structure the classroom so that students will be motivated to learn as much as possible.

- Build positive relationships with your students and colleagues. When others perceive you positively, you increase your influence and make it more likely that they will be receptive to what you have to offer.

- Develop clarity regarding what you want, your internal world picture. Look at the "big pictures" (What are my goals as a teacher? What are my goals for this school year?) as well as the day-to-day details (What do I want from today's lesson? If the students behave the way I would like, what will I see and hear? How will I know if my lesson is a success?). The more specificity you create regarding what you want, the easier it will be to select the most effective strategies from your repertoire to achieve it.

- Because there are so many variables over which we have little or no control, teachers frequently feel frustrated. Burnout is a serious problem that can compromise or ruin a potentially wonderful career. Instead of getting "stuck" on uncomfortable and unhelpful feelings, focus on what actions and thoughts you can select that will increase your effectiveness. The shift in emphasis to acting and thinking will free you from the paralyzing effects of negative emotion. Most importantly, you will discover that when you act and think in more effective ways, your negative feelings will dissipate and be replaced by more enjoyable feelings.

- Above all, focus your energy and attention on your own behavior. Instead of directing time and energy—precious and limited resources—toward trying to *make* students behave differently, look inward and determine what *you* can do (individually and collectively as a school) to increase your effectiveness with students. The more time and energy you spend looking at how to control others, the more you forfeit your control and effectiveness. The more you look inward and take responsibility for what *you* do (regardless of what those around you choose to do), the more you retain control and increase your effectiveness as a teacher. This does not mean that you don't care what colleagues, students, and parents do. Rather, it's an acknowledgment that they are responsible for their choices and you are responsible for yours. Clarification of the lines of responsibility, coupled with honest self-evaluation, will help you act like the educator you would like to be more consistently.

Teach Routines, Rituals, and Procedures

Learning something new renders us vulnerable, at least temporarily. Vulnerability can bring fear, an emotion that inhibits effective learning. For this reason, it is essential that teachers create an educational environment that is safe and secure, meeting one of their students' basic needs. The predictability of routines, rituals, and standard procedures enhances learning. In classrooms with inadequate structure, students are not sure what is coming next. Lack of predictability leads them to attend to all incoming information indiscriminately, rather than focusing their attention and energy on the academic task at hand. When there is sufficient predictability in the environment, students feel secure and are free to attend to what is most important. Classrooms with sufficient predictability allow students to feel safe enough to take the risk necessary for substantial academic growth to occur.

This chapter examines the importance of routines, rituals, and procedures in creating an inspiring classroom.

Mrs. Costa

"OK, guys. I'm giving you 15 minutes to look over your book report before I collect it," Gayle Costa announced to her 8th grade students. "Be certain that you have all the required components, including your illustration. And for goodness sake, make sure you have your name on your report! If you finish in less than 15 minutes, you can bring the report to me at my desk and take out some work that will keep you quietly productive."

As Mrs. Costa circulated among her students to make sure everyone was on task, Chad raised his hand. "Yes, Chad?" his teacher asked.

"Mrs. Costa, where do you want us to put our names? Do we need a special heading?"

Mrs. Costa herself had a strong need for freedom, so she tried as much as possible to provide that freedom to her students. She dismissed Chad with a wave of her hand, saying, "Don't worry about it, Chad. Just make sure your name is on each page. I don't care about a special heading. Worry about the important things."

"But should we put our names on the front so you can see it, or do you want it on the back?" Chad persisted.

"Chad," answered Mrs. Costa, slight annoyance in her voice, "I just said I don't care. Focus on the important things and stop fretting over something trivial."

Eight minutes later, Chad finished checking his book report. He joined a few other students in line and waited patiently to give it to Mrs. Costa. When he returned to his seat, Chad took out his binder and opened it to the science section. On top was his most recent report with a notation from Mr. Pearson, his science teacher, that his grade had been reduced from an 87 percent to 77 percent because he had used an incorrect heading.

Predictability Leads to Security

Gayle Costa's interaction with Chad illustrates several important points. In her effort to provide lots of choices for her students, Gayle unintentionally overlooked the important role that predictability and routine play in the classroom. Many students are like Chad. Driven by a high need for safety and security, they thrive when they know exactly what is expected of them and what they must do to succeed. The unintended outcome of Gayle's attempt to provide freedom for her students is that Chad feels less secure in her classroom. A well-ordered, predictable classroom is consistent with the principles of internal control psychology and is the foundation of an inspiring classroom.

Like many teachers, Gayle has a teaching style that matches her need profile. She has a strong desire for freedom, so she attributes that same desire to her students. Although a number of students do share her strong drive for freedom and will flourish under such circumstances, it is important that she considers ways for *all* students to satisfy their needs in order to succeed to their potential. Teachers who are strong visual learners often unknowingly create classrooms that are more compatible with the needs of visual learners. By the same token, teachers who are strong auditory learners typically create classrooms that favor auditory learners. The same is true of kinesthetic learners. Just as teachers should make sure that they instruct in a way that is inviting to students with different modality preferences, teachers should consciously make sure that their teaching is inviting to students with different need strength profiles.

If you are not careful, your attempt to build a classroom based on the principles of internal control psychology can result in significant problems. Specifically, teachers intent on providing freedom and infusing fun into the classroom often find there is more chaos than quality, and they quickly become disillusioned. To avoid that potential pitfall, begin by establishing order, predictability, routine, and ritual into your classroom. A well-ordered, structured classroom is the necessary foundation upon which to build a need-satisfying classroom.

At first blush, the emphasis on order and routine may appear to be at odds with internal control psychology. In truth, our need for safety and security demands adequate order and routine to maximize learning. Ritual and routine—stalwarts of predictability—help students feel safe and secure because they know what to expect. When we don't know what's coming next, we shift into a state of hyper-alertness, giving equal attention to all incoming information. Our primary goal is to remain safe. Teachers want students to concentrate on relevant input and to be driven by the need for power and competence because the development of skills is of paramount importance in the classroom. In a predictable, nurturing environment, students feel safe and secure and can comfortably direct energy toward increasing their academic competence.

Eric Jensen (1998, p. 50) suggests that we create learning environments that balance ritual and novelty. By its very nature, novelty is scary. When we don't know what something is, it could be dangerous. All learning falls under the category of "novel." When we undertake something new, we are initially unskilled. Because we are born with a drive to be competent, part of us strives to avoid novel situations and works ferociously to remain in our comfort zone, where we can perform with success and meet our need for competence. This is especially true for individuals with a strong need for safety and survival.

At the very least, learning demands that we experience a period of vulnerability and relative powerlessness when we encounter something new. This occurs all the time in challenging academic environments. What factors allow students to accept new challenges and embrace experiences that may bring failure? The answer depends upon the individual. Students with adequate self-esteem as learners and a high need for power are more likely to accept academic challenges, even though this runs counter to the drive for safety and security. Because they have a history of success, they are not unduly intimidated by the challenge novelty brings. Those whose drive for safety and survival is not especially strong can also easily accept novelty. Because students in this group naturally tend to be risk takers, they are more willing to take a chance even if they might fail, at least temporarily.

Some students, however—probably the majority—will be wary when asked to leave their comfort zone and make themselves vulnerable. This group is willing to take on new challenges only if the environment is predictable enough to make them feel secure. Given rituals and routines, these students will begin to feel that the classroom is a safe place, allowing them to accept new challenges despite their natural fear and hesitancy.

A challenging and rigorous academic experience provides considerable novelty in the form of new learning. The amount of novelty your students can effectively manage is directly proportional to the amount of ritual and predictability you infuse into your classroom. When students feel safe and secure, they are more likely to take risks precisely because it feels less risky! They operate with the perception that whatever happens in class, and however vulnerable they make themselves, they are always safe and secure.

The importance of establishing routines is emphasized by Harry and Rosemary Wong, who identify "the lack of procedures and routines"—not discipline problems—as "the number one problem in the classroom" (1998, p. 167). In fact, discipline problems multiply in a classroom that lacks order and routine. Creating appropriate order through the use of routines and established procedures will prevent many discipline problems, and prevention is always substantially more effective than even the most successful intervention.

Routines and Rituals

In keeping with Jensen's suggestion that we create classrooms that include a balance of ritual and novelty, make sure that your class doesn't become so ritualistic and predictable that it deteriorates into mind-numbing boredom. That said, all classes would do well to include a healthy dose of the predictability provided by ritual.

It is not necessary or even prudent that all of your classroom rituals be catchy, gimmicky, or fun. While they can include playful elements, effective rituals can be task-oriented, such as beginning your class with a "problem of the day." This strategy is easily employed in math class to review important concepts, but it can be applied to any subject. The ritual asks students to immediately get to work on a problem (or several) posted at the front of the room upon entering the class. As the students are engaged for three to five minutes and transitioning into their learning personae, you can attend to some of the other important details that are part and parcel of good teaching, like taking accurate attendance or checking in with any students who might have been absent the day before and giving them some quick instruction on what they need to get up to speed.

An end-of-the-week vocabulary quiz is another example of a ritual, as is a standard Monday night homework assignment. In all these cases, you are creating predictability, something that helps students feel safe, secure, and ready to take on increased novelty and learning.

Other rituals can be established regarding how you ask the class to quiet down, turn in assignments, label their work, leave the room, and so on. Because ritual has the potential to become boringly repetitive and tedious, be sure to include a few "lighter" rituals as well. Possibilities include a brief time on Monday morning when students have an opportunity to share something they did for fun over the weekend or an established time every week when several students are given the chance to tell an appropriate joke. While you don't want your classroom to cross the line into "cute," maintaining an atmosphere that is inviting and enjoyable supports learning. Positive rituals foster both the order you crave and the joyful atmosphere you need to inspire academic engagement and high achievement.

Procedures

Procedures refer to how you do certain things on a recurring basis. There is a seemingly endless list of tasks that are performed repeatedly in a typical class. The following is meant to be representative, not an exhaustive list:

- Taking attendance
- Passing out materials for class
- Collecting classwork, homework, and other materials
- Turning in late assignments
- Organizing handouts in a binder/folder
- Following rules for talking in class
- Asking permission to leave the room (to go to the nurse, restroom, etc.)
- Disposing unwanted material
- Borrowing a pen or pencil
- Lining up for dismissal
- Transitioning smoothly from one activity to another
- Arranging furniture for a particular classroom activity
- Behaving appropriately when a visitor comes to the classroom

I'm sure you can think of other tasks you and your students perform on a regular basis. Use the preceding list as a guide to get you started, and customize it so it accurately reflects your classroom.

Teachers are very busy. With the myriad curricular demands placed upon them, teachers often fail to take time to teach students to effectively and efficiently engage in routine tasks. This is especially true for secondary school teachers, who naively believe that students "should know how to do these things now that they are in the upper grades." As the story at the beginning of this chapter illustrates, however, not every teacher wants things done the same way. Some readers were undoubtedly appalled that Gayle Costa told Chad it didn't matter where he put his name on his book report. Mr. Pearson, Chad's science teacher, clearly wanted papers headed a certain way. Even teachers who are on the same academic team don't always have a common set of expectations. With that in mind, it is crucial that teachers identify those behaviors that are engaged in regularly and how they want those managed.

While it will take time to teach students how to pass in material or ask permission to use the restroom, once students have learned how to do things efficiently, they will have considerably more time to learn, and you will have considerably more time to teach. I supervised one teacher who used one of four different room arrangements, depending upon what she was teaching and her objective for the lesson. Because she invested time in teaching her students how to quickly arrange the room in traditional rows, four-person learning teams, a circle, and a horseshoe, they were able to arrange themselves the way she wanted in under a minute. Supported by a room configuration that matched her teaching objective, she was more effective in the delivery of instruction, and her students learned more easily. Furthermore, because each room configuration corresponded to a different set of expectations, the students knew immediately what was expected of them as soon as they arranged the room in a particular way. They knew that when they were sitting in rows with their seats all facing the front of the room, they should be quiet while their teacher gave direct instruction. When they were sitting in a circle, it was time for a class meeting or discussion. Because each room arrangement signaled a set of predictable behavioral expectations, the students behaved well and experienced academic success.

Internalizing new behaviors takes practice. Researchers differ about how many times a behavior must be practiced before students "own it." Moreover, learner variability means some students can learn a new routine with just a few repetitions, whereas some of their classmates need additional practice. In addition to the number of repetitions needed to learn, timing is a factor. Charles Hargis suggests that "limited amounts of repetition spaced over several days are more effective than the same amount of repetition concentrated in one period" (1995, p. 46). Given variations in learning style, ability, and other factors, it may be most prudent to practice important routines "until all students have achieved 100-percent mastery," as suggested by my colleague Jon Erwin (2004).

The Importance of Consistency

Let's revisit the story at the beginning of this chapter. We saw Chad return to his seat and look at the science report, on which he had lost 10 points for not putting his heading in the format Mr. Pearson wanted. How often have we heard teachers justifiably complain that they are given conflicting directives from different supervisors? "Why can't they get it together?" we complain. "We waste so much time around here because the administration isn't even on the same page."

Our students face the same frustrating contradictions on a daily basis, especially in middle and high school, where students have multiple teachers with different expectations and routines. Chad was criticized by Mrs. Costa for asking about something "trivial" like a heading after being penalized by another teacher for not having the right heading! Unfortunately, this happens often.

It is important for teachers to work cooperatively and develop a common set of expectations for as many routine behaviors as possible. It takes valuable time to teach students how to hand in their materials. If two or three teachers use the same process, the time it takes to teach important, albeit "trivial" routines will be cut dramatically. As a result, teachers will "waste" less time teaching routines and have more time for valuable academic instruction. And students like Chad will be less likely to be penalized for failing to remember too many different and arbitrary routines. There is no need for every teacher to adopt the exact same procedures for all routine behaviors. However, creating as much consistency as possible while allowing each teacher to have adequate autonomy makes good sense and promotes a sense of safety and predictability.

Summary

When we infuse our classrooms with ritual and establish specific routines and procedures for repeated behaviors, we make it easier for students to feel safe and secure. With this basic need addressed, students have the emotional energy to turn their attention to the primary goal of education: developing academic competence. A safe, predictable classroom is an essential component of making students feel comfortable enough to take the risk inherent in all new learning.

Getting Started

- Use ritual in your classroom to promote a sense of predictability and safety. Remember that the more predictability there is in the classroom, the more novelty (new learning) your students will be able to accommodate.
- Be certain that some rituals are enjoyable. While many rituals can be task-oriented ("problem of the day," weekly quiz, etc.), you don't want the classroom to become overly scripted, monotonous, and devoid of joy. Include some positive, fun rituals for balance. For example, you may give students a brief time at the beginning of each week to share something enjoyable they did during the weekend.
- Because rituals provide consistency and predictability, they support effective classroom management. It is especially important to have rituals at the beginning of class, at the end of

class, and during all times of transition. It is equally important to establish a consistent procedure to get students quiet and attentive. In addition to promoting safety and security, these rituals reduce unproductive academic time and help you maintain an instructional pace that promotes increased learning.

- Identify important routines and teach students how to effectively and efficiently engage in these behaviors. The time you invest teaching students routine behaviors such as entering and leaving the classroom, answering questions, getting necessary materials, and asking permission to leave the room during class will save considerable time during the school year.

- Create as much consistency as possible within an academic team or school. While individual teachers understandably want to maintain their autonomy, an academic team or whole school would be wise to adopt as much consistency as possible. A school culture that is united on how to handle tardiness, accept late assignments, move safely throughout the building, behave in the cafeteria, exit the building, and so on will establish a feeling of security and predictability that promotes higher achievement.

6

Be Enthusiastic and Enjoy What You Do

Teachers lucky enough to work with an energetic, enthusiastic principal certainly appreciate it. A positive outlook sustains the staff even in the most difficult times. Having colleagues with a positive attitude makes coming to work more enjoyable and fosters a climate where everyone is more productive. Just as negative energy can bog a school down, positive energy and enthusiasm for teaching enhance performance.

It's easy to lose energy and enthusiasm over time and slip into "been there, done that" mode. Even if you have been teaching for a long time, remember that the information you are sharing with your students is *new for them.* What we do becomes so habitual we can lose sight of the fact that we are opening up new horizons for young minds each and every school day. To fully engage your students, maintain your enthusiasm and make it clear that you enjoy what you do. What we do matters. Don't let the day-to-day minutiae dampen your enthusiasm for teaching.

Make it a point to enjoy your job and enjoy your students. Always remember that you are engaged in one of the most important and gratifying professions imaginable. Let your passion and energy for what you teach be evident to your students. Enthusiasm is contagious.

Mr. Blair

DeShawn and Kayla lingered by their lockers as the bell signaling the start of fourth period rang. "Let's go, guys," said Lenny Blair. "You don't want to be late. This is worth the price of admission."

"We'll be right there, Mr. B.," answered DeShawn, as he stuffed a few more things in his locker and the two students hurried into class.

As I watched the class get started, several things struck me. First, the walls of Mr. Blair's 9th grade English classroom were covered with exemplary student work. While some high school classrooms seem antiseptic, this one reeked of student involvement and high-quality work. Second, the change in student behavior as the class was about to begin was impressive. Just a few seconds ago, there had been loud voices and an almost raucous atmosphere, but once Mr. Blair shut the door, the atmosphere of the room shifted. As he approached the front of the room with a dramatic, energetic gait, the students fell silent and gave him their full attention.

"So," he began, "remember when you were in elementary school and you wrote haiku? Wasn't that one of the most enjoyable writing experiences you ever had?" The students signaled their agreement. "Beyond enjoying the experience, does anyone remember anything about the characteristics of haiku?" asked Mr. Blair.

"That's when you write with so many lines and so many syllables, right?" offered DeShawn.

"I remember that you had to follow these strict rules, but it was pretty awesome once you figured it out," added Carla.

"Great! That's all we need to get started," said Mr. Blair. "If you think that was awesome—and it was!—what we're about to do is going to be even better! Haiku is interesting, but it's pretty simple. That's why you got introduced to it in elementary school. Now," said Mr. Blair, lowering his voice for dramatic emphasis, "you're getting older, in high school, and ready to tackle something infinitely more complex—and interesting." The students sat up, alert to Mr. Blair's every word, waiting to find out what he was about to introduce.

"The sonnet," he intoned, "is one of the most demanding—and therefore most interesting—forms of writing. Who knows what a sonnet is?" Silence.

"No one? Even better! Now you get to play literary language detectives!" Mr. Blair exclaimed. "I'm going to show you several sonnets. Your mission—which I'm sure you'll decide to accept—will be to identify the characteristics of a sonnet. In other words, what makes a piece of writing a sonnet? When I give the signal, I want you to get into your three-person learning teams. You are not allowed to use a dictionary or any other reference materials. Every team will be given the same five sonnets. You will have 10 minutes to identify as many characteristics of a sonnet as you can muster and then craft a definition for the class to consider. Remember, you aren't being asked to read the sonnets for meaning. I'm not interested in the content at this point. Just the characteristics that lead us to identify a piece of writing as a sonnet." Mr. Blair paused, his eyes scanning the room to make certain he had the students' full attention.

"Now, to make this already awesome activity even more fun and challenging, here's what we will do. Your definitions will be written on a blank 8½-by-11-inch piece of paper. I will collect them all. I will then add the real definition, taken from our class dictionary, and I will read each definition. Your job is to write the most accurate, formal-sounding definition of a sonnet that you can, replicating the tone of our class dictionary. Ready? Begin!"

With that, the class quickly moved into their learning teams and began examining the five sonnets they had been given. In the next 10 minutes, I was treated to the sight of a class of 9th grade students actively engaged in sorting through the pieces they had been given and trying to figure out what made a sonnet. Interestingly, groups spoke in hushed voices, making sure that other groups didn't eavesdrop and "steal" their ideas. At the conclusion of 10 minutes, the groups turned in their definitions and prepared to discuss the sonnet, ready for and interested in what Mr. Blair was about to teach.

Just before the end of class, Mr. Blair quieted the students. "Today you played detective, and you are leaving the room smarter than when you walked in. Pretty good stuff. Tomorrow, you will take on a new role. Armed with your newly acquired knowledge, you will begin to create your own sonnets, proving that high school students are capable of manipulating language with skill previously thought to be possessed only by honored and long-dead authors. A splendid time is guaranteed for all!"

"What do we have to write about?" asked one student.

"Won't it be, like, next to impossible?" asked another.

"Relax, current detectives and future authors," answered Mr. Blair. "Too much stress will undoubtedly clog your brains and render you useless for tomorrow. You'll hear all about it tomorrow. Suffice it to say that you will be allowed to work individually or in pairs. As for subject matter, anything is fair game, as long as it doesn't violate school board policy or pose a threat to my job security or your disciplinary record. In other words, there will be lots of choice. Most importantly, you will leave here more competent than you are now and continue the exciting adventure of becoming educated young men and women." At that moment, the bell sounded, and an engaged group of 9th grade students filed out of the room with smiles on their faces.

The Students' Perspective

When I caught up with DeShawn, Carla, and Kayla later that day, they were happy to wax poetic about Lenny Blair. "That guy is, like, the best teacher I ever had," exclaimed Carla. "He just makes it so much fun to come to class."

"I'm especially interested in what makes Mr. Blair a successful teacher. And," I added, "it's important to know if he's a good teacher or just a popular teacher."

"I'd say he's both good and popular," said DeShawn. "It's easy to see that he's popular. He always gets listed in the yearbook as one of the most popular teachers in the school. So that's a slam dunk. As for 'good,' I don't know exactly what you think makes a teacher good."

"Give me your definition," I countered. "I'm curious to know what a high school student would define as 'good.'"

"Well, it's like the class you watched," answered DeShawn. "We had to come up with as many characteristics of a sonnet as we could discover and then make up our own definition. To me, a good teacher is one who gets kids excited to be there and working hard. Mr. B. definitely fits the bill." Vigorous nods from both Carla and Kayla signaled their agreement with DeShawn.

"So what does Mr. Blair do to get everyone to work hard and be excited to be there? What makes him different from other teachers? Or is he different?"

"Are you serious?" asked Kayla. "He's way different."

"Give me examples."

"That's easy. Maybe you noticed that DeShawn and me were a few seconds late getting into class. Mr. B. could have given us a tardy pass or made some big deal out of it like most teachers would. He just told us to get into class and reminded us it would be 'worth the price of admission.' End of story. He didn't threaten us with a detention. He talked about the class being worth going to. It's a whole different way of talking to kids. Instead of walking in all angry and stressed, it was no biggie. Because he cuts us a little slack, no one would ever take advantage of him. It would be so uncool. And then he's just so into everything he does. You just get excited because he's so into it."

"Exactly," agreed Carla. "I'm not trying to be mean or anything, but there are lots of teachers who seem like they are bored out of their minds. They carry around these ancient notes that look like they're made out of papyrus or something and ready to disintegrate. They have no enthusiasm for what they are doing. It's like they are just going through the motions and waiting for the day to end. It's depressing to be around them."

"Is that really common?" I asked.

"It's, like, the rule, and Blair's the exception," offered DeShawn. "Carla nailed it. A whole bunch of teachers seem like they are ready to pass out from boredom. But Mr. B. turns it upside down. Like today, with that whole detective thing he did. He was into it, so I got into it. And it was way more interesting to play detective than have some bored-out-of-their-mind teacher give you a bunch of characteristics and definitions to memorize."

"I saw that everyone was engaged during the lesson," I agreed. "But suppose it hadn't been something so interesting?"

Kayla rolled her eyes as she said, "In case you didn't know, learning about the characteristics of a sonnet and writing a definition worthy of a dictionary are not exactly on the list of 'most interesting' to your typical 9th grade students. What made the lesson work was Mr. Blair's energy, passion, and enthusiasm. When we see him so into it, we get into it. It's contagious."

"I'd like to add something," said Carla. "I'm not sure I agree with DeShawn that most teachers are bored. A lot of teachers are pretty passionate about what they do. Mr. B. is kind of over the top, as you might have noticed, but other teachers show that they really care about what they teach. I think that's huge for me. If you want to teach me anything, I need to feel like it matters to you. Otherwise I'm not really interested in listening. But you don't have to be super-dramatic like Mr. Blair. As a matter of fact, if some other teachers tried it, it might not work because it's not who they are. Mr. Blair pulls it off because he's always genuine—even when he's being his most outrageous self."

"Yeah," said DeShawn. "I guess I was a bit harsh. We have other teachers who are less animated than Mr. B. but still show they got passion for their thing. And Carla's right. Students need to know that you dig your stuff if you want them to dive in."

"Do any of you want to add anything?" I asked.

"I do," said Carla. "I'm not sure if this fits exactly, but one of the things I really like is when teachers take us seriously and listen to our ideas like they matter. It's like they're so interested in learning that they pay close attention to the students because some comment might add to what they already know. When you're really into your subject, you can learn things even from your students because kids sometimes have a whole different way of looking at things. So I think teachers who are most passionate about learning and have a lot of enthusiasm are receptive to ideas brought up by the kids. And that would be a good dictionary definition of Mr. Blair." Kayla and DeShawn nodded their assent.

Mr. Blair's Teaching Philosophy

My meeting with Lenny Blair that afternoon surprised me. Based on his classroom persona, I had expected a display of energy bordering on hyperactivity and an effusive personality. Instead, I was sitting across the table from a somewhat reserved, reflective high school English teacher.

"We're all multifaceted," he began, fully aware he was presenting a very different side of himself. "What you saw earlier today was Lenny Blair, energizer of potentially turned-off freshmen. My mission is to excite and inspire, and I have to display a fair amount of enthusiasm or it's over even before I've had a chance." He paused for effect, just as I had seen him do in class. "I'm assuming I don't need to adopt the same role in order to have a productive conversation with you."

"Agreed," I said. "You're not saying what I saw was an act, are you?"

"Not at all," he answered. "If nothing else came through to you and the students, I hope at least everyone left appreciating that I'm into my subject and into teaching. No, I'm not faking it in class. I am, however, intentionally selecting how to present myself and the material to the kids."

"What dictates how you present?" I asked.

"I learned a long time ago that the kids feed off whatever energy the teacher puts out. I intentionally exaggerate my enthusiasm to get the kids into what we're doing. I know they think I'm a little nuts. That's absolutely OK with me. See, my goal is to inspire as many kids as possible and to help every kid be competent in English. If the most effective way for me to attain my goal is to be borderline insanely enthusiastic, that's fine. I'd rather my students think I'm nuts, learn a lot, and be inspired than have them think I'm a perfectly normal guy and that English is a drag."

"The students intimated that you were in the minority, that most of their teachers seemed to lack your passion and enthusiasm. Would you agree?"

Lenny sat quietly for a few moments and then said, "Your question seems straightforward enough at first, but there are really two distinct issues. Am I more passionate than most? I doubt it, and I hope I'm not. I'd like to believe that all teachers have passion about their subject and about the art and science of teaching. It would be naive to think that's true for everybody, but I suspect the vast majority has real passion for what they do and what they teach. So I don't agree with the passion part.

"I would, however, agree with the enthusiasm part. I've taught for nearly 20 years, and I've been in several school districts in a couple of states. I've been around enough to say that many teachers don't think displaying enthusiasm for the subject is part of the job. I do."

"Tell me more," I encouraged.

"I can't tell you how many teachers I've met who are crystal clear that they have no interest in entertaining the students. They say things like, 'Hey, Blair, you want to be an actor, go ahead. If I wanted to be an actor, I would have found an agent and got my Actors' Equity card. I'm a teacher. I teach. Those who want to—learn. Those who don't—fail. It's called responsibility and accountability.'"

"I take it you disagree," I said.

"Again, it's not that simple. On one level, I have no argument with that viewpoint. Part of me would love to simply stand up there and pontificate while an eager group of students hung on every word. That just hasn't been my experience!" Lenny said with a laugh. "And I'm kind of stuck, because I want what I want, and that's hardworking, engaged learners. I discovered a long time ago that I had a better chance of reaching my goals if I brought energy and enthusiasm into my classroom every day, even on days when I might be dragging. I'd rather generate enough energy to excite my students than be a bitter, unfulfilled teacher who complains that kids *should* work harder. And this issue goes way beyond the kids and whether they are being responsible or being held accountable. It's more about me taking responsibility for my professional life and holding myself accountable for being the teacher I want to be. It's me deciding who I want to be regardless of what's going on around me and not getting sidetracked because the world isn't always the way I think it *should* be. Being enthusiastic about what I do helps me be more successful." Lenny paused, then added, "Plus, it's way more fun!"

Commentary

In my career of more than three decades, the complaint I heard more often than any other from students was, "This is boring." Truth be told, too many teachers structure their lessons and classrooms as if they agree. Lenny Blair and countless others like him provide evidence every day that passion and enthusiasm are contagious. Present information to your students in a way that suggests the subject is tedious and only marginally interesting at best, and you will fail to inspire. You may "get through" your classes, but it will be hard to enjoy yourself in such a mind-deadening environment.

Bring substantial energy to your classroom—about both your subject and the magical enterprise called teaching—and most students will follow your lead and immerse themselves in what you teach. In all likelihood, you won't inspire the majority. Only a fraction of students will be inspired by any given subject. But when you bring energy and passion to your teaching, you give yourself the opportunity to inspire some students and help the vast majority develop the competence we want for everyone. When you do that, you will be more successful as a teacher and enjoy your chosen profession immensely.

Unfortunately, what Lenny Blair said is true. Our faculty rooms are full of unhappy colleagues who grumble that too many kids just don't work hard enough, that parents and communities aren't supportive enough, and that teaching shouldn't require us to engage and entertain. If complaining about such unfortunate realities were effective, the problem would have disappeared decades ago. Rather than sentence yourself to a career marked by disappointment and bitterness, you can choose to put your passion and enthusiasm on display for your students and begin to get results that will make you proud to be a teacher. As Lenny Blair indicated, we all decide who we want to be.

Getting Started

- Infuse your teaching with energy and enthusiasm. While you may not be an entertainer, your energy will be contagious. Don't forget that one of your primary responsibilities is to inspire your students. Enthusiasm is one of your most effective tools.

- Choose your words carefully. Instead of saying, "This next concept is very difficult," tell the students, "I expect you will enjoy what we're doing next. It's a real challenge, and you'll have every reason to be proud of yourselves when you've mastered it." When students ask, "Why do we have to learn this?" don't tell them, "Because it will be on the test." Use their natural inquisitiveness as a reason to share why what you are teaching is exciting and worth knowing. Don't be afraid to promote what you teach!

- Remember why you decided to teach what you teach. Put your excitement for the subject matter and the process of teaching on display.

- Strike from your vocabulary anything that gives the impression that what you are about to teach is tedious and boring. When you present information to students with that orientation, you have already lost the majority of them.

- Part of the drive to belong and connect includes a tendency to agree with others. When you teach without passion, students follow your lead and put little effort into their work. When you teach with energy and enthusiasm, your students will likely take on the same positive attitude toward learning.

Build Positive Relationships with Students

Education is fundamentally a process of human interaction. Although high-quality content and instructional plans with clearly identified learning objectives are essential, they are not sufficient to guarantee high achievement for all students. If you create need-satisfying, positive relationships with your students, they are more likely to engage academically and achieve more. When you develop a positive relationship with your students, they feel connected, are able to demonstrate competence, are provided some choices, and have fun in a safe environment. Creating and maintaining positive relationships with your students involve more than simply liking each other. A positive relationship also includes developing an environment characterized by trust and respect.

This chapter will take a look at the crucial role positive working relationships play in both classrooms and schools.

Turning Passion into Positive Relationships

Used effectively, the passion and enthusiasm exemplified by Lenny Blair in Chapter 6 can engage your students. However, in the absence of a positive interpersonal relationship, passion and enthusiasm can interfere with the goal of high student achievement. Teachers who show enthusiasm for their subject matter but demonstrate little interest in their students as individuals will inspire only those students who happen to have an affinity for the subject—typically only a small fraction of the class. Therefore, exhibiting enthusiasm exclusively for the subject matter is not especially helpful if you want to reach all learners.

There are some teachers who have such passion about student achievement and want so much for their students to be successful that their emotional energy causes problems. Such a teacher often becomes excessively frustrated with students who fail to work to their potential and "don't realize that they are wasting their lives and limiting their options by doing less than they should." The teacher has such a strong picture in his or her internal world about how students *should* behave that he or she creates emotionally charged perceptions. When the students are less engaged and productive than the teacher believes they should be, frustration and negative emotion drive the teacher's behavior, frequently leading to a coercive relationship rife with criticism. Such relationships disengage students rather than encourage them, despite the teacher's positive intentions. If you find that your vocabulary is peppered with "should," your perceptions are significantly fueled by your values, and you are prone to interactions marked by conflict because things are frequently not the way we believe they "should" be. To avoid the disappointment that can accompany a strong value filter, adopt an orientation like Lenny Blair's. Lenny kept himself from growing disillusioned and maintained positive energy for teaching by focusing on those things he could control. He displayed a passion for teaching and brought energy into the classroom every day, regardless of what his students did. If Lenny had focused more on his students' behavior rather than his own, or if his behavior was dependent on what the students chose to do, he would have had less control and been more subject to becoming frustrated, disillusioned, and bitter.

Do You Like Your Students?

Some years ago, I conducted a multiday workshop with a teacher who was well versed in the principles of external control psychology but receptive to learning a new approach. An avid learner, Liz Langlois freely admitted that she had a lot of discipline problems with her 5th grade students. "Especially the boys," she said. "They are so immature, silly, and off task. They have no clue that what we're doing in our English language arts class provides the foundation for the rest of their educational future. It is so frustrating to watch these boys waste valuable time and lose ground every day." Not surprisingly, the students' frequent disruptive behavior resulted in substandard achievement as well.

As we talked, I asked Liz about her relationship with her students, especially the boys who were the most disruptive. "Do you get along well with them?" I asked.

"When they behave appropriately and do their work," she answered. Although she was not consciously aware of it, Liz had a conditional relationship with her students. She only enjoyed them when they acted the way she wanted them to. This put her in a difficult position, because students frequently fail to live up to our expectations. Passionate, dedicated teachers like Liz who create relationships that are contingent on students meeting their high expectations leave themselves vulnerable to disappointment.

"From what you've said, Liz, oftentimes they are off task and not doing their work. Let me ask you a simple question: Do you like the kids?" I asked.

With no hesitation and complete candor, she answered, "I didn't think that was part of the job." Liz made this comment without rancor or embarrassment. Liking the students was simply something she had not considered particularly important to being a successful teacher.

I was stunned; for a moment, I didn't know what to say. I remember vividly the strong visceral reaction I had. "Not only do I think it's part of the job, Liz," I began, "I think it's absolutely essential that you like kids and develop a positive relationship with them if you hope to be an effective teacher. While I'm not saying that a positive connection with your students will make you a great teacher, you can never hope to be a great teacher without the foundation of a strong relationship." Liz sat passively and looked at me with bewilderment.

Liz was a passionate teacher. She wanted her students to thrive and succeed academically because she valued learning and academic success. Unfortunately, her enthusiasm for academic excellence blinded her to an essential element in educational success: we need to develop a positive relationship with our students if we want them to engage in the highest-quality academic work.

The first step in creating a positive relationship with students is simply liking them and accepting them as they are. There is a fundamental difference between teachers and students. Teachers are adults who choose to be in school voluntarily. Students are youngsters whose school attendance is generally mandated by law. Part and parcel of effective teaching is realizing that the inappropriate behavior we sometimes witness in the classroom is perfectly appropriate from a developmental perspective. While good teachers don't condone off-task behavior, they never let undesirable student behavior erode a positive working relationship. Regardless of what the students do, successful teachers retain an abiding appreciation of kids and genuinely like them.

Whereas routines and procedures address the need for safety and survival, positive relationships help us meet the need to belong and connect. When we build positive relationships with our students, we make our schools need-satisfying. Because people are more productive in a need-satisfying environment, positive relationships support the academic mission of the school.

The correlation between positive relationships and productivity is reflected by a phrase I saw on a homemade poster in Michelle Greene's classroom. The poster read, "Open your hearts; free your mind." When I saw it, I asked Michelle to explain why she had chosen this motto for her class.

"I want all of my students to learn as much as possible," she replied. "I want them to free their minds and take risks and be excited about learning. They can't do that until we open our hearts. Learning includes risk. Kids will only take that risk when we have created a caring classroom community. To get the kids to 'free their minds,' I need to make sure they 'open their hearts.'" Michelle is successful in part because she intentionally creates and maintains a positive relationship with all of her students. Moreover, as a professional, she knows the difference between being friendly and being friends. She is welcoming and positive with her students even when they "don't deserve it" but makes it clear that her role is to be their teacher, not their friend.

A positive working relationship requires that you establish boundaries, articulate expected behavior, and clearly identify the roles of both teacher and students. Students can easily misinterpret the friendly behavior of their teacher and forget that school is a place for hard work. Developmentally, youngsters see things simplistically and often erroneously believe that if you treat them nicely, there will be no demands put upon them. To make sure that a friendly relationship does not compromise learning, establish guidelines and expectations as soon as the school year begins. Let the students know what behavior will be sanctioned and what is off limits. Help them understand that being *friendly* doesn't mean you are *friends.* Discuss your role and their role with them. Even primary grade students can partake in a conversation about what everyone in the room needs to do to make the class successful. In fact, these conversations help children assume an appropriate level of responsibility. They begin to see at a very young age that they are active participants in the educational process and that success is dependent upon their actions and choices. Creating a shared vision of appropriate roles and behaviors in an enjoyable, productive class helps build a positive relationship without compromising academic integrity.

Information does not come to us in a vacuum; it is delivered by a person. How we perceive the deliverer of information affects how receptive we are to the new information. If students perceive you in a negative light, they will be less likely to take in and retain the new information, even if you identify it as "essential" or "good for them." When their perception of you is favorable, they are much more likely to take in the new information and develop a richer, more accurate perception of the world. When you like your students, they will be more receptive to the valuable information you have to share with them as a teacher. Positive relationships create an environment that fosters high achievement.

It is so essential that teachers perceive kids positively that I made investigating this concept a central part of the interview process when hiring new staff. With few exceptions, the candidates I met all had the requisite pedagogical skills and came prepared with impressive portfolios and in-depth lesson plans that identified learning objectives and referenced the state standards addressed by their proposed lessons. From a technical perspective, virtually every candidate I met had "the right stuff." It didn't take long to discern in an interview if the candidates liked kids or not. Surprisingly, for many applicants, the kids were an afterthought. They were in love with their subject. They were smitten with teaching. But they had very little interest in kids. Regardless of their technical expertise, I steered clear of any applicant who did not clearly demonstrate that he or she liked kids and was enthusiastic about the ways that teaching allowed him or her to assist youngsters in the process of growing into responsible, productive adult members of our community. If the applicants didn't truly enjoy being with kids—even with all their antics—they would be unable to succeed in the classroom with the vast majority of students.

Do Your Students Trust You?

I frequently tell the story of Lynn Wilson, a 2nd grade teacher in Sandwich, Massachusetts, where I live. An outstanding teacher, she creates positive relationships with her students, and the students trust her completely. When my daughter Melanie was in Mrs. Wilson's class many years ago, she was given a homework assignment. I asked Melanie if she thought it was important to learn about fractions, the topic of the assignment. She assured me that it was very important, "because Mrs. Wilson said so!" While Melanie may not have been able to appreciate that understanding fractions would be important later in her life, her total trust of Mrs. Wilson led her to do the kind of quality work we wish all students would do.

It's no accident that more students experience success in elementary schools, where the relationship between teachers and students is generally deep and positive ("deep" because students typically spend most of the day with one teacher, and "positive" because young children are typically more driven to establish and maintain a positive connection with their teachers). The emphasis on content and subject matter and the de-emphasis of the student–teacher relationship in secondary schools contribute to the disengagement and academic decline we typically witness. With all due respect to Mrs. Wilson, it's generally much easier to win the unwavering trust of 2nd grade students than that of middle and high school students. Still, I have worked with numerous gifted teachers over the years who experience success with their students because they have proven they can be trusted. Building a relationship of mutual trust not only supports our need to belong; it also supports our need to be safe and secure, fostering an environment that is predictable.

Do Your Students Respect You?

I spent much of my career as a school psychologist. I vividly remember testing Gerard, a 3rd grade student. As I always did when testing students, I asked Gerard if he liked his teacher. "Yes!" he told me, with typical 3rd grade enthusiasm. "He's great!"

"Tell me what makes him a good teacher," I continued.

Gerard was silent, and a look of consternation spread across his face. "I'm not sure if he's a real good teacher," he told me with some hesitancy, "but he'd sure be fun to have as an uncle!"

Even though Gerard was only 8 years old, he was savvy enough to distinguish between liking his teacher and respecting him. While he undoubtedly liked his teacher, there was a lack of respect that I suspect had a negative impact on how much Gerard learned that year. Students generally don't put forth maximum effort with teachers they don't respect.

In contrast, my son Greg had Don Morrison as a teacher in the 6th grade. One time, Greg turned in a take-home test a day late. Mr. Morrison surprised him by saying, "Do you want me to correct this?"

"Sure," answered Greg, clearly confused by the question. "Why are you asking?"

"Well, it was due yesterday, so you will not receive any credit. I just wanted to know if you were still interested in the feedback."

When I was informed about the incident, I asked Greg if he was upset about receiving no credit.

"Well, sure I am," he said. "But it's not like I'm mad or anything."

"Tell me more," I urged my son.

"Mr. Morrison would do the same to anyone in the class. He doesn't play favorites. I mean, I know he likes me, but that doesn't mean I can get away with not turning things in on time. I'm mad at myself for turning in the test a day late, but I'm not mad at Mr. Morrison, because he treats everyone the same way and he explains everything ahead of time."

Like all great teachers, Don Morrison earned the respect of his students. While there's no simple formula for earning respect, Greg identified how important it was to him that his teacher didn't play favorites and treated all students fairly. I am also confident that the students respected Mr. Morrison because his actions spoke loudly about how much he respected his profession and himself. He was always available for extra help. He did not abuse sick time. He didn't give the kids a lot of "free time," believing that educational time was too valuable to be squandered. Rather, Mr. Morrison made his classroom engaging and fun and at the same time, challenging and productive. Because of his actions, he not only commanded respect. He earned it.

Don't Look for a Recipe

A positive relationship is not something easily summed up with a vignette. It is multifaceted and built over time. Although there is no recipe for creating a positive relationship with your students, there are a number of items on the "menu" that you can select to build the kind of connection with your students that will help you both succeed. Listed below are a few suggestions:

- Send a brief welcome letter to students before school begins, letting them know that you are looking forward to working with them. (Note: This strategy is especially effective with elementary school students.)

- Get to know students in the lower grades. If you have already established a positive relationship with students before you have them in class, they will enter the class with a positive perception of you. (Note: This practice is particularly effective with secondary school students.)
- Host a "step-up day" for incoming students who will be part of your school community the following year. This helps ease the transition to a new school and can function as much more than a simple orientation to a new building. You can use it as a time to begin creating positive connections with incoming students. To that end, make sure to make this event positive so the students are excited about coming to school the next year.
- Greet students by name when they enter the room.
- Attend student games or events.
- Learn something about the students as people with lives outside the classroom. Similarly, let the students know something personal about you. When they perceive you as a person with interests, friends, and a life outside the school, they will relate to you on a personal as well as professional level and be less likely to behave inappropriately. In *The Classroom of Choice* (2004, p. 51), Erwin describes a teacher test you can give students at the beginning of the school year that will allow them to get to know something about you and begin to build a positive working relationship.
- Spend some time at the beginning of the school year on team-building activities designed to create positive connections in the classroom. (Note: If you focus on positive connections only at the beginning of the school year, you will be less successful. Maintaining positive connections should be an ongoing theme in your class.)
- Acknowledge personal events like birthdays, athletic awards, and so on during the year. Such acknowledgments need not be time-consuming, and they remind everyone that students have lives outside the classroom.

All of these things—as well as a host of other factors—lead students to feel that you are someone to be liked, trusted, believed, and respected. The students will know that you have their welfare in mind when you ask them to do something.

There is no surefire formula for creating a positive relationship with your students. While there are certain commonalities to a good working relationship, we all have to find our own way, because relationships must be genuine, reflecting our individual style and personality. When you develop a positive working relationship with your students, they will work hard and behave appropriately (at least most of the time). There will be mutual respect and a shared vision of what it means to have a successful class.

Substantial research affirms the strong link between positive relationships and high academic achievement (Leachman & Victor, 2003; Marzano & Marzano, 2003; Schaps, 2003; Sullo, 2007; Tate, 2004). It doesn't matter whether you believe in the principles of internal control psychology that I advocate or are a proponent of the traditional reward/punishment model. Either way, a positive relationship with your students will increase your effectiveness.

Certainly, students achieve more when positive relationships exist in the classroom. But there's another reason to develop positive relationships. Quite simply, you'll enjoy teaching more! In our conversation, Liz Langlois admitted that she was deriving far less joy from teaching than she wanted and had expected. Is it any wonder? Because she didn't even consider that liking the students was "part of the job," she did little to develop the positive relationships with students that make going to work every day a joyful experience. Each day she faced the very predictable "silly" behavior that is part of what it is to be a 5th grade boy, and she was both frustrated and unhappy. Exacerbating the situation was the fact that Liz was not yet 30 years old! She expected to teach another 25 to 30 years. If she does not find a way to develop positive relationships with her students and enjoy her job more, she will be doomed to a woefully unpleasant, unsatisfying career. When you create positive relationships with your students, you are likely to experience considerably more pleasure and satisfaction while simultaneously increasing your effectiveness as a teacher. Just ask Michelle Greene, who urges her students to "Open your hearts; free your mind." Because she develops positive relationships with her students, Michelle maintains her love of teaching and enjoys her chosen profession immensely. Just ask Lenny Blair. His energy and enthusiasm help him create the positive relationships with his 9th grade students that result in them being excited about learning how to write a sonnet.

The Positive Relationship Trap

When students engage in high-quality work just because they like and respect you, they are operating from an external orientation, and we have already seen that we need to move beyond that to internal motivation. If Melanie works hard in math only "because *Mrs. Wilson* says so" and she has a less positive relationship with her teacher the next year, she will not work as hard or do as well. If you want kids to put working hard and learning as much as possible into their internal world, then a positive relationship is an essential starting point—but it is not the end of the story. Help students move beyond working hard for you to a point where they work hard because they appreciate that working hard and learning as much as possible enhance their lives.

It's easy to become self-satisfied when students work hard for you, even if they *are* operating from an external orientation. Like everyone else, you have a drive to be competent and powerful. Naturally, when your students work hard and succeed, you feel good. However, when you consciously create a picture in your internal world of students working hard and achieving because they value learning for its own sake, you will no longer be satisfied with students working hard just because they have a positive relationship with you. You'll want something more, something deeper. You will be left unsatisfied when kids achieve only because of you. Of course, you'll want to foster and maintain a positive relationship with your students. And you'll understand that the positive relationship you develop will be the foundation upon which to build. But you won't be satisfied until you can help your students move beyond an external orientation and develop a deep-seated love of learning and achievement. In addition to creating a positive relationship with you, help your students develop a positive relationship with the subject matter, their peers, the school, and learning.

Think about the teacher you want to be. Do you want the students to work hard just because they like you, or do you want them to develop a genuine passion for learning and achievement? If you want them to develop a passion for learning in its own right, make sure that you consciously attend to what will help them move in that direction. Use your positive connection with your students to nurture the thirst for learning.

A Connected Community

While the relationship that I have stressed in this chapter is between teacher and student, consider the other relationships that exist within a school. Specifically, think about the relationships among students, among staff members, between teachers and paraprofessionals, between teachers and building-level administrators, and between teachers and parents. In every case, positive relationships enhance the smooth and effective functioning of the school. Problems in any of these areas negatively affect both morale and productivity and interfere with student achievement.

Begin by defining what a positive relationship would look like in each of the areas just described. Work intentionally on maintaining or enhancing relationships to positively affect student achievement. Ideally, this would be a collaborative effort that solicits input from all involved parties to collectively define the kinds of relationships you want to create in your school community. To simplify the process, allow yourselves to be guided by the following question: "What will make the school a joyful, successful organization?" With a shared vision front and center, a staff can come together and commit themselves to more productive, satisfying relationships that serve the students and enhance their educational experience.

We spend considerable time at school. Those teachers who have positive relationships with their students and the adults who make up the school community enjoy their jobs significantly more than those who have failed to nurture positive relationships. The double benefit of creating positive relationships is that they not only make our jobs more enjoyable but also enhance students' academic achievement.

Getting Started

- Identify what you currently do to build positive relationships with your students, and make a commitment to continue those behaviors. It's easy to abandon effective practices unless we intentionally commit to maintaining our successful strategies.
- Enjoy your students! In all likelihood, a fair portion of the unwanted behavior you encounter is developmentally appropriate. While you shouldn't tolerate disruptive behavior, don't let "typical" behavior interfere with your love and enjoyment of children. Keep things in perspective, and remember you are dealing with "works in progress."
- Be certain to distinguish between being *friendly* and being *friends*. Your effectiveness as a teacher is supported by being friendly with your students, because we all perform better for those we like. Your role as a teacher does not involve being friends with your students. Establish and maintain a positive but professional relationship with your students.
- Make sure your students can trust you. Follow through on what you say you will do and cultivate the reputation that you can be trusted. Trust enhances relationships and supports a safe, predictable environment. If students feel that you cannot be trusted, it damages your credibility and compromises your effectiveness.
- Be certain that your students respect you. One way to earn respect is to give it unconditionally. Teachers who respect students "only when they deserve it" are seldom respected. Those who decide they will be respectful regardless of how students behave quickly earn the respect of their students.
- Identify at least three additional things you could do that would improve your relationship with students. Implement at least two of them.

- Assess your relationships with other adults who make up the school community (teachers, paraprofessionals, administrators, parents). Identify at least two things you will do to enhance those relationships in a way that will improve your job satisfaction and success. Begin to implement strategies to enhance your relationships right now.
- Never forget that your ultimate success as an educator will be largely determined by the quality of the relationships you form with everyone who makes up the school community. Make positive relationships a priority.

Create Relevant Lesson Plans

Because we are continually bombarded with incoming information, our brains naturally screen out what is perceived to be less essential, attending most closely to what is judged to be important. Unless we are careful, students can screen out a lot of academic input before they even have a chance to consider it.

To increase the likelihood of students attending fully to the input you are providing, make the information need-satisfying and help them see its relevance. When students perceive something as important and relevant to them, they are considerably more apt to give it their full attention, creating the necessary conditions for maximum achievement.

Connecting your lesson to the lives of your students increases their motivation and supports achievement. This chapter tells how one math teacher helped her students get excited when learning about the concepts of mean, median, mode, and range.

Ms. Ortiz

One fall Monday, a group of 6th grade students entered Trish Ortiz's math class.

"Let's check it out," Josh said. "The Patriots only scored 24 points yesterday. I wonder what that will do to the mean!"

"Josh, you know it's going to bring it down," said Max.

"How do you know that?" asked their teacher as students made their way into class. On the whiteboard at the back of the room were the New England Patriots scores from each of their first nine games:

38, 38, 38, 34, 34, 48, 49, 52, and 24. After each football game, Trish Ortiz posts the scores and uses them to help her students review the concepts of mean, median, mode, and range, which are included on the annual state math assessment for 6th grade students in Massachusetts.

"I know," answered Kelly. "Since 24 is their lowest point total in any game this year, it has to drop the mean."

"What else does Kelly's comment tell us?" asked Ms. Ortiz. "Cassie?"

"Since it's their lowest total, the range changes," Cassie answered.

"Tell me more. Be specific," the teacher urged.

"Before, the range was from 52 to 34," continued Cassie. "Now it goes from 52 down to 24."

"Good. Max said the mean would drop, and we've established he's right, because the range has been extended downward. The Patriots have played nine games so far," Ms. Ortiz continued. "Pretend they had the same nine scores but in a different order. Suppose they had scored 24 in game three instead of in game nine. What can you tell me? Austin? What do you think?"

"I know if they had the same nine scores, the range, mean, and mode would be the same," Austin answered.

"What's the mode?" Ms. Ortiz asked.

"Thirty-eight," said Austin.

"How do you know?"

"Because it's the score that appears the most," Austin replied.

"Would the mean have been impacted the same way if the Patriots had scored 24 points in game three after scoring 38 in both games one and two?" Ms. Ortiz asked. "I want you to figure out the mean with the nine scores we have and then calculate the mean if the first three scores were 38, 38, and 24. Let me know what you come up with in the next two minutes. It's okay to use your calculators."

While the students immersed themselves in this task, Ms. Ortiz took attendance and had a brief conversation with two students who had been absent the previous day. Then she turned her attention back to the whole class.

"Okay. What did you come up with?" Ms. Ortiz began.

"I've got it," said Chantelle. "In the nine games that they've played, the mean is 39.4 points."

"Agree?" Ms. Ortiz asked the class. "If so, give Chantelle a thumbs-up." The 24 students in the class all indicated agreement. "Go on, Chantelle."

"But," Chantelle added, "if the Patriots had scored 24 points in the third game of the season, then the mean at that time would have been only 33.3 points."

"Let me know if you agree with Chantelle," Ms. Ortiz said. "Let me see those thumbs." Again, all students agreed. "What does all of this tell us? Mike?"

"A really high or low score will change the mean more if there have been fewer games," Mike answered.

"Who can connect this to the projects you are doing for science?" the teacher asked.

"That's why you told us we needed to have at least 20 people in our survey," answered Kara. "I'm doing mine on what flavor of ice cream people like most. If I just asked four people, then one person would make a huge difference. By having at least 20, one person doesn't change my results so much. It's like it's more honest."

"I'm not sure it's 'more honest,'" countered Ms. Ortiz. "Both the examples you gave are 'honest.' But having a greater number increases the chances of your results being more reliable when you consider the general population. So let's go back to mean, median, mode, and range for a minute before we move on. I want you to take out your math journal and write three to five sentences that capture what you have learned from this discussion. Please be sure to write in complete sentences."

As soon as the directions were given, all the students took out their journals and began writing. Throughout the brief review of these essential concepts, which students sometimes find tedious, the class had been engaged and attentive.

Ms. Jenkins

Just a few doors down the hall, another group of 6th grade students made their way into their math class somewhat more slowly.

"You see the game yesterday?" Marcus asked his buddy Mitch.

"OK, guys. The weekend is over. Time to get focused on math. You can talk all you want about the game when you get to lunch," Sandra Jenkins said dispassionately. The two boys looked at each other, rolled their eyes, and ambled slowly to their seats.

"It's Monday morning," began Ms. Jenkins. "You know what that means. Time for our weekly review of mean, median, mode, and range."

"Why do we have to know this stuff?" Amy protested. "It's boring."

"You're going to be seeing it again in the spring when we have our state assessments," explained Ms. Jenkins. "My job is to get you ready to excel, and your job is to make sure you know your stuff. Now let's stop the complaining and get to work. I'm going to give you a series of numbers, and I want you to identify the mean, median, mode, and range for each set. Okay. Here you go." She then went to the front of the room and wrote the following numbers on the board: 38, 24, 49, 52, 17, 75, 6, 27, and 9.

For the next seven minutes, the class reviewed the concepts of mean, median, mode, and range with little energy and even less emotion, accompanied by furtive glances around the room and occasional yawning.

The Students' Perspective

After Trish Ortiz's math class, I had the opportunity to talk with Max, Cassie, and Austin.

"I'm interested in your opinions about Ms. Ortiz's class," I began. "Anyone care to share your thoughts?"

"Sure," said Cassie. "I think Ms. Ortiz is awesome. She finds a way to make school interesting and not boring."

"Exactly," chimed in Max. "Like, today is the perfect example. We review mean, median, mode, and range every week. You saw how she uses scores from the Patriots. It just makes it interesting. I know this sounds kind of weird coming from a 6th grader, but I actually look forward to coming into class Monday morning to check all that stuff out."

"We all know kids in other classes," Austin added. "Every math teacher reviews this stuff every week. It's to make sure we're all prepared for the state tests. But I have friends in other classes who tell me how deadly boring it is when they review. For us it's pretty awesome. I'm into sports and really like statistics. This helps me understand it better, and that's important for me because I plan to be a general manager of a sports team someday."

"Aside from being enjoyable," I continued, "do you think you learn as much as or more than kids in other classes?"

"I bet we do at least as good as the other classes," offered Max. "Probably better."

"What makes you say that?" I asked.

"It only makes sense," said Cassie. "When you enjoy something, it's going to be way easier to learn it. The classes I think are boring are always the ones I struggle in. When it's interesting, like in Ms. Ortiz's class, it's easier to learn."

"I'm curious about the things Ms. Ortiz does to make class relevant for you. I know she does the football thing. Is that more successful with the boys? And are there other things she does to make it interesting?"

"I'll answer that one," said Cassie. "I know some people think sports is just for guys, but girls like sports just as much. Just because we don't play football doesn't mean we don't find it interesting, so I think sports things work pretty good with just about everyone. Even the kids who aren't really into sports don't mind it because we don't even talk about football or the game. She just uses those numbers because she knows a lot of us watch the games so it's more interesting. They aren't just numbers, if that makes any sense."

"Plus," added Austin, "Ms. Ortiz always connects what we're learning with what we're doing in our other classes. Like today, when she started talking about the surveys we are doing in science. So it's not like we're doing math for no reason. She helped us see that having more people in our science survey makes it more reliable, just like the mean changes depending on how many games have been played. She's always connecting what we're studying to something that's real to us. So no one ever asks, 'Why do we have to do this?' She makes it obvious."

"Do you have other examples?" I asked. "I'm looking for things I didn't see today but that she does on a regular basis."

"You probably know that we have to do a lot of word problems in math," Max began. "When Ms. Ortiz gives us problems, she always makes them about us! So it's like we have to figure out how many lawns Austin will have to mow to get a new MP3 player or how much baby-sitting Cassie has to do to buy tickets to a concert. Figuring out problems about kids in the class makes it more real and more fun. It's like, no one really cares how much 25 times 5 is, but when you know that Austin needs $125 to get that MP3 player and he gets $25 when he mows a lawn, it makes it interesting. It's information we can actually use."

"Thanks. This has been helpful. Any last comments that you want to make?"

"I think everyone really appreciates that Ms. Ortiz takes the time to make learning fun and something we can relate to," said Max. "And one more thing. Nobody is going to beat the Patriots this year. You can put that in your book." Several months later, it became clear that Max's final comment could be attributed to the unfailing, naive optimism of youth!

Ms. Ortiz's Teaching Philosophy

I spoke with Trish Ortiz later that day.

"I was impressed by how you created a math lesson that the students found relevant. Is that difficult to do?" I began.

"Not really," Trish replied. "In fact, it's easier than doing the same lesson without including a way for the kids to connect to what I'm trying to teach. I know that concepts like mean, median, mode, and range can be tedious for kids, and unless they have a way to make it 'real' and interesting for them, I'll never get their best work."

"Tell me what you mean when you say it's easier," I said.

"It doesn't take any additional effort to choose numbers the kids can relate to, like the number of points the Patriots score. And by doing that, I have a class who sees the connection between math and things they enjoy in the 'real world,'" explained Trish. "It would be considerably more difficult to get the kids energized and motivated if I used a random group of numbers, so this is easier."

"Well, it certainly appears as if the kids enjoyed the class. The ones I spoke to had lots of complimentary things to say," I said.

"That's nice, obviously," Trish said with some hesitation. "I'm glad the kids find the class interesting, but the bottom line for me is how they perform. I take my role seriously, and if the kids thought I was the world's coolest teacher and voted me as their favorite every year, it wouldn't mean much if I didn't help them develop their skills. That's my job, and all the 'relevance' I infuse into my classroom is done because I know it supports learning. I don't do it just so I can say my lessons are 'relevant.' There has to be a purpose for what I do. Having happy students who like me is a bonus, but having competent students is essential. This way works for me."

Without trying to be contentious, I asked, "How do you know it works?"

"That's simple," Trish answered. "I don't want to sound like I'm bragging, but my kids routinely score better than their peers on our state tests. I am proud of their results. No one can talk about teacher bias or grade inflation when the data we're using are standardized state assessments. And because it has happened consistently for the past seven years, it can't be attributed to luck or simply getting a good group of kids one year. That's what I take pride in. I know that by making sure that I connect what I'm teaching to the lives and interests of my students they increase their proficiency and skills."

"Do you have any idea why every teacher doesn't do what you do?" I asked.

"Truthfully, no," answered Trish. "I know that some teachers get caught in a power struggle with kids and are very hung up on kids accepting responsibility for their own learning. While I have no argument with that concept, I'm way too pragmatic and selfish to get caught in that game."

"Tell me what you mean," I urged.

Trish smiled. "Basically, I'm selfish," she said. "A lot of people think I make these huge accommodations for the kids that involve all this extra work on my part. Like I said, the truth is it doesn't take much time at all to inject something into a lesson that helps kids connect to it and see it as relevant. Seriously, what could be more relevant than math? I just make obvious to kids what is so obvious to me: the things we're learning *are* relevant and meaningful. Once they see that, they get engaged and learn more."

"You identified yourself as selfish. In what way?"

"Because when my students routinely outperform their peers, I feel good about myself. It affirms that I am a competent professional, and that means the world to me. It matters to me to be good at what I do, and making my lessons meaningful to my students lets me be the most successful math teacher I can be."

"I wouldn't call that selfish, Trish," I said. "We all have a need to be powerful and competent. You feel powerful by working *with* your students, as opposed to some teachers, who exert power *over* their students. You are not being selfish. I appreciate your time, Trish. Is there anything else you'd like to say before we finish?"

"Yes, there is. I know a lot of my colleagues think that it's a waste of time and coddling kids to create plans that they can relate to. I wish they knew that it is not a time-intensive process and that anything that helps kids advance academically is time well spent—not a waste of time. And as for coddling kids, I see myself as someone who helps kids see what they can't see on their own. That doesn't seem like coddling to me. That's just good teaching. And by the way, if you check it out, you'll discover that my students don't do any better than their peers on their report cards! I may be nice. I may make my lessons relevant. My students may learn a lot. But I've never been accused of being an easy grader!"

Commentary

Studies have demonstrated that students better retain and apply what they have learned when it is connected to real-life experiences (Westwater & Wolfe, 2000). Trish Ortiz is an exemplary teacher because she intentionally creates lessons that are relevant and meaningful to her students. Compare the activity in her class with what was going on in Sandra Jenkins's classroom down the hall. Because Ms. Jenkins made no effort to make the learning relevant to her students and infused no emotion into her instruction, the students worked with little energy or enthusiasm. As Thomas Armstrong (2006) writes in *The Best Schools*, "If a student ... is told exactly what to learn, read, study, and memorize, then it is likely that the student will not be motivated" (p. 125). He goes on to say, "During early adolescence, it seems clear that the curriculum needs to ... engage the students' feelings in a gripping way" (p. 129). Creating lessons that students perceive as relevant is especially important in middle school. Elementary school students are typically driven primarily by the need to belong and connect. For that reason, relationships with their teacher and classmates are of particular importance. High school students are frequently more goal-oriented as they prepare for life beyond high school graduation, whether it be employment, the military, or college. Middle school students, more than any other group, need to connect to what they are being asked to learn. As Armstrong suggests, "Whatever the lesson might be, teachers should always attempt to link it in some way to the feelings, memories, or personal associations of the students" (p. 129).

According to Trish Ortiz, it's easy to deliver instruction that engages students and increases their level of motivation and achievement. While some teachers bristle at the suggestion that they should make their lessons meaningful and show students the relevance of what they are being asked to learn, Tomlinson and McTighe (2006) state, "Learners of all ages are more likely to put forth effort and meet with success when they understand the learning goals and see them as meaningful and personally relevant" (p. 121). With a few simple strategies, teachers can engage students, inspire increased motivation, and cultivate greater academic achievement.

Getting Started

- Take time to show students how they can use what you are teaching. One effective practice is to inform the students of the "real-life" implications of what they are going to learn at the beginning of a unit of instruction. At the conclusion of the unit, have students demonstrate their new knowledge by applying what they have learned. For example, as an introduction to a unit, you may explain that scientists and engineers use certain elements of physics and aerodynamics when creating aircraft. At the end of the unit, the students can be asked to create paper airplanes that travel the farthest distance and explain how they constructed them using the information that was taught during the unit.
- Whenever possible, ask students to compare what they are studying to experiences in their own lives. As Armstrong (2006) suggests, this is particularly important for middle school students. Questions like "How is this similar to or different from your life?" or "In what ways does this remind you of something in your life?" provide opportunities for students to relate to the material personally.
- In any subject that involves people, personalize the experience with questions or comments like the following: "Imagine you were friends with the main character. Would you be pleased or disappointed with what she did? Why?" "Pretend you were an advisor to the historical figure we are studying. What advice would you offer him to manage the problems he faces?" "Imagine some of the things we have been studying had never been invented. How would your life be different today? In what ways would it be better?"

- Relevance can be created even when the situation is unrealistic or imaginary. For example, you can ask students to answer questions like these: "Pretend you had to be either a verb or an adjective. Identify which part of speech you would rather be, being careful to explain exactly what you do compared to the other part of speech." "Imagine you are one of the first 10 amendments to the U.S. Constitution. A vote will soon be taken that will determine if you are going to be eliminated. Write a first-person account justifying why people should vote to keep you in the Constitution. Remember, your very existence depends on this vote, so include specific reasons why you are important enough to be maintained!" When students inject themselves into these scenarios, they become more engaged and interested in developing convincing arguments.
- Students are inundated with input on a daily basis. Make certain that the information you present gets past the brain's natural screening device by making it meaningful to your students. Be explicit in helping students see how immersing themselves in what you are teaching will benefit them.

Create Realistic Expectations

Our basic need for power drives us to seek competence. Even though our schools are plagued by too many students who struggle to succeed or seem not to care, no one *wants* to fail. Power and competence can only be attained when we develop new skills and competencies as a result of legitimate effort. When academic tasks are too easy, students may enjoy the good grades they receive, but they can't meet their need for power without exerting themselves. For this reason, it's essential to provide an academic experience that is sufficiently challenging.

At the same time, students need to believe that success is within their grasp if they put forth sufficient effort. When students think that they cannot succeed even when they try, their drive for power typically leads them to seek power in less responsible ways, such as class disruption and the adoption of an "I don't care" attitude.

Successful teachers offer an academic experience that is challenging without being overwhelming. Through ongoing, formative assessment and differentiated instruction, they identify an appropriate "instructional zone" for each student so that all students are challenged but have the opportunity for legitimate success with reasonable effort.

Because of the innate drive to be competent, it is crucial to create classrooms where students believe they can attain success with reasonable effort. This chapter shows what happens to a teacher and a student who are put in a situation where they have no chance to succeed.

The Favor

Imagine that you have been teaching high school English for 12 years. You are competent and well respected, and you thoroughly enjoy your job. One day during the summer recess, just a couple of weeks before school is scheduled to open, the principal calls you at home and asks you to drop by at your convenience in the next several days. He says he has a favor to ask. You have a reputation for doing whatever is asked to help the school function smoothly and effectively.

When you arrive at the school the next morning, you are completely unprepared for what the principal has to say. "We have a bit of a problem," he begins. "Actually, it's more of a major problem, but I think I've come up with a solution, if you can help me out."

"Sure," you say. "You know I take pride in doing what's necessary to make things work around here. What do you have in mind?"

"As you know, it's very difficult to get qualified math teachers on the high school level. Even though I've had several positions posted for quite some time, I still have one unfilled math position."

"I'm not sure what that has to do with me," you say. "I've put out the word, but I don't know of anyone we can snag for a math position."

"Well, there are a number of qualified English teachers out there looking for work. My idea—and I've already spoken with the superintendent, and she thinks it's got great merit—is to have you teach math this year. I can get a highly qualified candidate to take an English position for just one year and return you to your English position next year."

The look of bewilderment mixed with terror on your face speaks volumes, so the principal hurries on. "Look, I know you're not a math teacher, but you're a *teacher*. And a damned good one. A great teacher can teach anything. And it's just for a year. I promise."

"But I'm not even licensed to teach math!" you protest. "Besides that, even if I were, I'd be horrible!"

"First, you wouldn't be horrible," the principal says, interrupting you before your protest can continue and gain momentum. "Sure, you might struggle, but you'd do a decent job. As for the licensing aspect, we don't have to worry about that. The superintendent is confident she can get a waiver to put you in the role for a year, since we've made a good-faith effort to fill the position. It's a hell of a lot better to put a veteran teacher—a competent teacher—in that math position than leave it in the hands of some unlicensed, unknown quantity. And with the luxury of time this move provides, I'm sure I can get a qualified math teacher next year." The principal pauses before adding, "You don't have to worry about doing a great job. I know and the superintendent knows you're bailing us out here, and we appreciate it. We don't expect you to teach math the way you teach English. We just want you to do the best you can. And I give you my word that you will not be given a poor evaluation. Just do your best, and we'll take care of you. What do you say?"

The quintessential team player, driven by your strong need for belonging and a desire to avoid conflict, you agree, albeit reluctantly and with full-blown trepidation.

The following year proves to be the least enjoyable of your teaching career. Although you felt both overwhelmed and unskilled when you were a first-year English teacher, that was nothing compared to your one-year experience as a math teacher. The principal does everything possible to make things better. He even relieves you of your daily duty period so you have an extra prep period. ("Call it a favor for helping us out," he says.) He is good about checking in regularly and telling you how much he appreciates your hard work and effort. When he thinks you are feeling particularly over-whelmed, he reminds you, "Just give it your best. Don't worry about how well you're doing. Just do your best. That's all we're asking, and you're giving us that every day." While you value the kind words and reassurances, they don't really help. You go to school day after day, month after month, feeling less competent than you want to, and your lack of competence tears you apart. Mercifully, the year ends, and the principal, true to his word, returns you to your position as an English teacher the next year, where once again you resume your successful career.

Unrealistic Expectations

Upon hearing the preceding story, most educators are appalled. "How horrible," they think, "to be asked to do something you know you can't do well and to have to face it day after day for a full school year." Even the promise that there will be no negative evaluation and the frequent gestures of appreciation and support by the principal aren't enough to assuage the unfairness of being asked to do what you simply can't do well. As professionals, we want to be competent. When we are subjected to an experience that promises long-term failure despite our best efforts, we are outraged.

Now consider this. In virtually every school, there are students who struggle mightily with the academic demands placed upon them. I'm not talking about students who lack the motivation and work ethic to succeed academically. I'm talking about students with legitimate learning deficits, learning disabilities, cognitive impairments, and other factors that prevent them from progressing at the same rate as their peers. While it may be nice to say that we can create classrooms where no child is left behind, the painful reality is that some students do not have the skills and cognitive wherewithal to perform at a competent level.

I began this chapter with a hypothetical story about you being asked to assume a teaching role in which you would be agonizingly aware of your inadequacy every day. As uncomfortable as that is, it is only a story. And the main character is a strong, successful, competent adult. And it only lasted for one year, with the fulfilled promise of returning to a role where success was attainable.

For too many students, this is not hypothetical. And they don't have the advantage of a success identity already in place. And it doesn't last for just one year. And there is no hope held that the situation will improve appreciably in the future. If anything, the achievement gap only widens over time for these students.

Imagine how disheartening it must be to be one of these students. And what do we tell them? "Just try." As if that somehow makes it OK and negates the sting of chronic failure. Paradoxically, it's exponentially more difficult to cope with failure after demonstrating great effort than it is to fail without trying. Many struggling students cease working hard and delude themselves into thinking that they could be successful with just a little effort. And we become coconspirators when we say that their failure is attributable to a simple lack of motivation. It's not that cut-and-dried. Yes, there are students whose failure can be attributed to simple laziness and a profound lack of motivation to achieve academically. But the vast majority of students who underachieve lack the fundamental skills to be successful.

I am reminded of Tim, a student I knew from my days as a school psychologist and adjustment counselor. When I first met Tim, he was a 2nd grade student who was receiving special education services. During my first meeting with him, I asked Tim if he liked school.

"No," he said.

"When did you start disliking school?" I asked.

"I've hated it since kindergarten," he replied. "I'm just no good at school."

I saw Tim again three years later as part of his special education reevaluation. He remembered me, so I asked, "School any better for you?"

"It's worse," he said. "I thought I was bad at it before. I'm even more bad now. I just wish I could quit." He was in the 5th grade!

Several years later, I saw Tim once again. It was in the spring of his 8th grade year, and the school was about to begin the annual ritual of state-mandated testing that would dominate everyone's time and energy for several weeks. "I might as well just quit school right now," Tim told me. "They can give me that MCAS [Massachusetts Comprehensive Assessment System] as many times as they like. I'm just never going to pass it. I'm not going to graduate, so I might as well just quit now."

Imagine. Thirteen years old. Tim was in the 8th grade and convinced he would never graduate from high school. Having evaluated Tim twice previously, I knew that his fears were not unreasonable. He did have significant deficits that would make passing the MCAS tests highly unlikely. Defeated in early adolescence.

What makes Tim's story even more disturbing is the fact that he had impressive intelligence in areas not typically assessed or valued by school. He told me with pride and enthusiasm how he could assemble and disassemble small motors and boasted, "I can build anything. I'm good with my hands." Despite our gratuitous enthusiasm for the concept of multiple intelligences, in most schools, if you are less able in the verbal and mathematical domains, you are on the fast track to failure. It would be bad enough if Tim were an aberration. Unfortunately, he is representative of an increasingly large number of students who are being systematically left behind because our expectations are unreasonable and unrealistic.

What happens to students like Tim, students who feel they can't achieve power and competence by being successful in school? Most of them don't sit there passively. They become disruptive and interfere with the learning of other students. It's not long before multiple students are negatively affected by these overwhelmed students. Ultimately, they are at greater risk for dropping out of school without graduating. The prospects for a high school dropout are not promising in the 21st century. And once again, we all pay the price, as dropouts are more likely to engage in criminal activity, become a drain on the legal system, and require costly social services.

If we provide students with an opportunity to achieve success and demonstrate competence when they show reasonable effort, virtually all students will become engaged, challenged learners who contribute positively to our classrooms and our communities. When we deny that opportunity to even a small minority, we have failed to do our jobs.

Commentary

While our academic expectations are reasonable for the majority of our students, a sizable minority come to school every day with little hope of ever experiencing success. Their initial disengagement quickly deteriorates into disruption, wasting valuable instructional time and compromising the learning of other students. Tomlinson and McTighe (2006) cite numerous studies that indicate motivation to learn is decreased when tasks are consistently too difficult for a learner. If we do not engage these overwhelmed students, the results will be devastating on multiple levels.

What steps can we take? First, identify that dynamic place where students are stretched but not broken. Create challenging learning environments, but make sure that the challenges can be successfully met with hard work. Differentiated instruction is essential. Every teacher needs to develop skills to be effective with a widely heterogeneous group. The work of Carol Ann Tomlinson (1999, 2003; Tomlinson & McTighe, 2006) is particularly relevant and will help you structure your classroom to keep academically disadvantaged students engaged.

One practice to abandon is grading students against each other—unless, of course, our goal is simply to rank and sort. Pitting student against student is highly effective when we want to separate the "winners" from the "losers," the "haves" from the "have-nots." Assuming we have moved past that antiquated notion and we recognize that not every student has the same ability, it is more appropriate—as well as more fair—to assess students by comparing their performance against their own previous performance over time. Not every student can achieve at the same level within the same time frame, but every student can make gains. Asking students to make academic gains regardless of their level of competence or cognitive ability is a reasonable challenge that every student can successfully meet with good instruction and hard work.

Traditional academic teachers can learn a lot from their colleagues in physical education. There is a long-standing tradition in phys. ed. that students compete against themselves, not each other. It is understood that not every student will be able to run a mile in seven minutes, but all students can be challenged to do their best and improve their performance. This doesn't "dumb down" the expectations and lead to decreased achievement. Elite athletes continue to push themselves to be the fastest runner in the school, the district, or the state. But less able runners take legitimate pride knowing that they run *faster* now than they could before. They don't resent those who are more gifted. They accept that not everyone has the same gifts in every area. As a result, they don't disrupt, they remain engaged, and they improve their performance.

We can apply the same practice in traditional academic classrooms. In *The Art and Science of Teaching,* Robert Marzano (2007) describes how using a simple rubric throughout a unit of instruction as we conduct formative assessment gives all students the opportunity to succeed without distorting their level of achievement or artificially inflating grades. Less able students can be recognized for their improvement while we honestly acknowledge that their performance level still lags behind most of their peers, Marzano's suggestion protects teachers from falling into the too-familiar trap of telling students they are "doing great" when their performance is still substandard. It prevents student and parents alike from developing erroneous perceptions about the student's level of competence. At the same time, tangible evidence of improvement helps academically challenged students remain engaged, especially when we communicate that we value the development of a strong work ethic more than we expect every student to be equally successful academically.

Finally, what we choose to report to students and parents on a report card reflects what we value. Even if we *say* that we value a positive work ethic and responsibility, traditional report cards in most secondary schools provide grades only in identified subject areas. The concepts of hard work and responsibility are embedded in the grade, but the fact that they are incorporated into the "real" grade is strong evidence that they aren't highly valued.

There is nothing that prevents us from providing grades in the area of hard work and responsibility. Doing so has a number of advantages. First, it is tangible evidence that we value these concepts enough to assess them. Second, it levels the playing field, because every student has the ability to succeed in this area. Third, it results in academic grades communicating more accurately what the student has accomplished. Currently, too many academic grades are "muddied" by the inclusion of effort, hard work, and responsibility. Students who work hard appear more academically able than they are, and their grades are artificially inflated because of their work ethic.

Students who demonstrate less effort may have their grade lowered and thus appear less academically skilled than they are. Both perceptions are erroneous and unintentionally mislead students, parents, future teachers, and prospective employers. When we start issuing a separate grade to students for their work ethic and responsibility, we will provide valuable information to these stakeholders while also giving every student a chance to be successful.

A grade for effort is necessarily subjective. Regardless of how objective we might like to be, it is virtually impossible to accurately assess how much effort a student has put forth on any assignment. Compounding the difficulty is the fact that low-performing students with poor self-esteem often give up easily. Does that reflect a lack of effort, or is it a coping strategy designed to blunt the pain of habitual failure? Because it is so difficult to know how much effort a student exerts, I suggest assessing students on responsibility and work ethic, variables that can be more easily defined and measured. Teachers can easily create a rubric that describes what students must do to demonstrate a positive work ethic and responsibility. For example, a teacher might consider if work is turned in on time and if assignments are complete and include all required components. Furthermore, teachers can assess if work is neat and presentable. Creating a rubric that defines the criteria for work ethic and responsibility and asking the students to evaluate themselves in these areas promote responsibility.

There are many reasons to assess students in the areas of work ethic and responsibility. First, it distinguishes these aspects from academic performance, which results in the academic grade being less ambiguous. Second, it communicates clearly to students that we think a positive work ethic and responsibility are important. Because these are areas where all students can succeed regardless of their cognitive ability, it gives every student an equal opportunity to be successful. Finally, employers frequently complain that new hires lack a strong work ethic and sense of responsibility. When we provide grades to students in these areas, we are more likely to overtly teach students how to develop the skills essential to being productive employees in the future.

If we take these steps, every student will have a legitimate opportunity to be successful, and we can create schools where no child will be left behind. The importance of developing realistic expectations for our students is stated eloquently by Tomlinson and McTighe (2006), who write: "Students are more willing to 'play the school game' if they believe that they have a chance to be successful. If we limit success *exclusively* to standards-based achievement, we are unwittingly disenfranchising those students who work diligently and make significant personal gains, yet are hampered by disabilities, language, and other barriers" (pp. 136–137).

Getting Started

- Part of creating realistic expectations is having standards. An all-nurturing classroom with insufficient rigor denies students the chance to meet their need for power through academic effort. Even less gifted students benefit from a classroom that requires effort in order to succeed, because that is how we responsibly meet our need for power.
- Create lessons and assessments that allow every student to be successful with reasonable effort. Because most classrooms include students with a wide range of academic ability, it is essential that you differentiate instruction. Effective differentiation results in every student being given an academic experience that is simultaneously challenging and manageable.
- Developing a classroom with realistic expectations requires you to define success differently from how it has been traditionally defined. In the past, success was defined as earning good grades. In an academically challenging classroom, only a minority had a chance of meeting the criteria for success. In a classroom where good grades were given for substandard performance, the grades were meaningless, and students felt no sense of accomplishment because too little was required of them. When success is defined as *improving your performance and demonstrating an increase in skills and competencies,* every student has a chance to be successful. More importantly, their

success is gratifying because it involves measurable improvement as a result of legitimate effort.

- Abandon the practice of grading students against each other or against standards that you know are unreasonable. Such ill-informed practices will lead to less able students giving up because they know they have no chance of being successful.
- Adopt the practice of grading students based on their current performance compared to past performance. Include each student's "current performance level" when reporting progress. It's important for students and their parents to know where they stand in comparison to grade-level expectations. When you don't clearly indicate if a student is performing at grade level, above grade level, or below grade level, letter grades can be unintentionally misleading.
- If you value hard work and responsibility, make them part of your formal grading system, and give them the same emphasis as grades for content learning. Many employers bemoan the fact that new employees seem adequately competent but lack the work ethic necessary to be successful. Part of our job as educators is to prepare students to succeed in the world of work. Grading students on work ethic and responsibility gives them valuable feedback that will serve them after their formal education has ended.

Plan with the Students' Needs in Mind

Successful teaching requires thorough preparation and lesson planning. In recent years, teachers have become increasingly vigilant about creating lessons with well-defined learning objectives. Identifying what students will learn and be able to do at the conclusion of a lesson maximizes instructional focus and improves teacher effectiveness. Thankfully, the days of teachers "winging it" are largely a thing of the past.

While academic content and defined learning objectives deserve time and attention, it is equally crucial to plan with our students' basic needs in mind. Students are more engaged and productive when they are offered need-satisfying academic activities. To maximize your success as a teacher, be certain that when students do what you want them to do, they can connect with each other, develop increased competence, make choices, and enjoy themselves in a safe, secure environment. When students can satisfy their needs by immersing themselves in the productive academic challenges you create, they will behave appropriately and perform better.

It is common for teachers to carefully consider content and learning objectives as they prepare their lessons. This chapter introduces a simple practice that will maximize your effectiveness by also addressing your students' basic needs as you develop your lessons. This equally important planning strategy will result in lessons that are need-satisfying, academically engaging, and successful.

A New Dimension to Planning

Our instructional practices have improved dramatically in recent years. The adoption of state standards and curriculum frameworks has resulted in more focused, uniform teaching. When I began teaching in the mid-1970s, it was not uncommon for teachers to teach what they liked. My students learned a lot about Greek mythology and Romantic poetry, primarily because those were topics I knew well and enjoyed teaching. My colleagues in the English department emphasized different topics. Standardization was nonexistent. Today, the curriculum is more uniform and delivered with greater precision. While some might argue that such standardization is too rigid, a mobile society that aspires to provide an equal educational opportunity to all students demands a level of uniformity.

Beyond improvements in curriculum, today's teachers are considerably more aware of the learning objectives for each lesson. In the past, teachers might be able to identify their agenda for the class, but they were less attentive to the desired learning objectives. Teachers knew what they were going to *cover*, but they weren't necessarily sure what they wanted their students to *learn*. It's not uncommon today to walk into classrooms and see precise, well-crafted learning objectives clearly posted on the board. This gives teachers and students alike a common understanding of where we're trying to go and what teachers want their students to know and be able to do at the conclusion of the lesson. Such clarity is essential to effective teaching, and we are remarkably better at this than in the past.

When I taught English, I stressed with my students that it is essential to know your audience when you write. The same is true in teaching. Our two areas of greatest improvement in teaching focus on the "what" (the content) and the "where" (the learning objectives) of teaching. It's important to know what you want to teach and where you want your students to go, but to maximize our instructional effectiveness, we need to structure lessons to meet the needs of those we teach (the "who"). Exemplary content and precise learning objectives are necessary but not sufficient. We also must provide instruction that is need-satisfying to our students so that they will be engaged and fully benefit from the wisdom we have to share.

Planning with the students' needs in mind is a simple and powerful process. Intentionally creating lessons and units of instruction that are need-satisfying and sensitive to what drives student behavior will help us reap the benefits of the gains we have made in curriculum and instruction in recent years.

One of the most valuable characteristics of this planning strategy is its simplicity. Teachers are busy enough. They justifiably complain about plates that are too full, and they have little interest in a process that is time-intensive. Planning with the students' needs in mind takes only a few minutes and provides a focus to your lessons that will enhance your effectiveness. After more than 30 years in education, I hesitate to make guarantees. However, if you take the few minutes needed to plan with the students' needs in mind, I guarantee that you will have fewer disruptions in your classroom, that disruptions will be more quickly managed to your satisfaction, and that your students will achieve more.

How can I make such claims? All behavior, including disruptive behavior, is purposeful. We behave to meet our needs. When lessons are structured so that students can meet their needs by doing what the teacher wants, there is naturally a reduction in off-task, disruptive behavior. Even in the best classrooms, there will be the occasional disruption, just as there are arguments even in the best of friendships. In the need-satisfying classroom, however, those rare instances of disruption are handled promptly, just as good friends generally resolve their differences quickly. In a need-satisfying environment, all parties are motivated to put any discord behind them and work together in productive harmony. Finally, because of the reduction in disruptive behavior, students in a need-satisfying classroom engage in more on-task behavior, leading to increased academic achievement—provided there is good instruction, a carefully crafted lesson, and clearly identified learning objectives.

Planning with the Students' Needs in Mind: The Process

Good teachers who have an agenda, a road map they use to reach the learning objectives at the heart of their lesson, will find that planning with students' needs in mind is quick and easy. If you teach on the secondary level and have the students for a class period, simply identify what you ask the students to do during a given class period and about how much time you think you will spend on each activity. The same applies to specialists at the elementary level who see students for a defined time block for art, music, physical education, and so on. If you are an elementary classroom teacher (or anyone else who has the students for an extended time frame or all day), pick any block of time (for example, from the beginning of the day until recess, from recess until lunch, from lunch until art). For that time block, identify what you ask the students to do and how much time you expect to spend on each activity.

Let's begin by looking at an elementary classroom from the time students enter the classroom until an hour later, when they go to a specialist. The plan book identifies what the teacher wants the students to do and about how long each activity will take. While time guesstimates are often erroneous because of unanticipated interruptions, they are still helpful. Imagine that the following activities are planned for the time block we are considering:

- Morning work: 5 minutes
- Circle time/sharing: 10 minutes
- Teacher reads aloud to whole class: 10 minutes
- Think-Pair-Share: 2 minutes
- Choice of three activity centers: 20 minutes
- Whole-class instruction: 8 minutes
- Transition/prepare for specialist: 5 minutes

In Chapter 4, you were introduced to the five needs that drive all humans:

- To survive and be safe and secure
- To connect and belong
- To achieve power and competence
- To be free and autonomous
- To play, enjoy, and have fun

We now need to determine if the proposed lesson will be need-satisfying for students. For maximum achievement and minimal disruption, it is essential that doing what the teacher wants allows students to meet their needs.

We do not have to explicitly address the need for power and competence, because everything we ask our students to do builds students' level of competence, assuming we provide a differentiated experience that gives every student a chance to succeed academically. Neither is it necessary to consider the need for safety and security, because in classrooms where students feel insecure and unsafe, teachers are generally aware of the problem and work diligently to address this serious impediment to effective learning.

We will look at the remaining three needs: to connect and belong, to be free and autonomous, and to enjoy ourselves and have fun. For each of the activities being considered, ask the following questions:

If the students engage in this activity the way I would like them to, will they

- connect with others and feel a sense of belonging in the classroom?
- have some choice about what they do and feel a sense of freedom and autonomy?
- enjoy themselves and have fun while being academically productive?

Note that it is *not* necessary for every activity to address every need area. In fact, that would be virtually impossible. What is essential is that students responsibly satisfy each need for some time by doing what you ask when they are with you. The fact that a given activity may not address certain need areas doesn't matter as long as the teacher is careful to ensure that each need is adequately addressed during the time being considered.

Figure 10.1 illustrates how the teacher planning the above activities might answer these questions. An "X" indicates that the students will satisfy that need when doing the activity. An empty box indicates the students won't meet that need at that time. The chart takes only a couple of minutes to complete, and the teacher then has a visual representation of how need-satisfying the proposed lesson will be for the students.

Figure 10.1 | Does the Activity Satisfy Students' Needs?

Activity	Time	Connect/ Belong	Freedom	Fun
Morning work	5 minutes			
Circle time/sharing	10 minutes	X	X	X
Teacher reads aloud to whole class	10 minutes	X		X
Think-Pair-Share	2 minutes	X	X	X
Choice of three activity centers	20 minutes		X	X
Whole-class instruction	8 minutes	X		
Transition/prepare for specialist	5 minutes			

What does Figure 10.1 reveal? Notice that only two activities address all three need areas. That doesn't mean that they are "better," will be more successful, or are more essential. Two other activities don't intentionally address any of the need areas. Most would agree that getting the students academically productive with morning work is important. It doesn't have to directly address the needs we have identified, because other activities during the lesson allow students to meet these needs easily. While the five-minute transition at the conclusion of the class does not intentionally address any of the listed need areas, either, a smooth transition at the end of class is part of exemplary teaching. Because the students have had so many opportunities to satisfy their needs by doing what the teacher has planned, they will almost assuredly be cooperative and responsible when it's time to get organized and transition to their specialist. If students have not met their needs during the lesson, transition time will be marked by chaos and disruption.

If the information the chart provides shows gaps in addressing students' needs, the teacher can immediately identify the area or areas that are underrepresented. This facilitates a proactive orientation and enables the teacher to take corrective action before initiating a lesson that would be less effective than it will be with minor revision. Figure 10.2 represents a potentially problematic lesson being considered for a secondary school classroom.

Figure 10.2 | Does the Activity Satisfy Students' Needs?

Activity	Time	Connect/ Belong	Freedom	Fun
Morning work/problem of the day	5 minutes			X
Review homework	10 minutes	X		
Quiz	10 minutes			
Introduction of new concept/ whole-class instruction	20 minutes	X		X
Begin homework/answer individual questions	10 minutes			

We can immediately see that the teacher has planned activities that make it easy for students to connect for 30 minutes and to have fun for 25 minutes. Even though only two activities in Figure 10.2 address those needs, they are sufficiently lengthy that students can satisfy these needs reasonably well while being academically productive.

However, a quick glance at Figure 10.2 shows that students cannot satisfy their need for freedom and autonomy by doing what the teacher has planned. This is not to say that the proposed activities are less valuable, but a lesson that offers no freedom to students invites problems. Fortunately, the teacher can utilize the information provided by Figure 10.2 to modify the proposed lesson, increase student engagement, and curtail disruption.

Teachers who do not plan with their students' needs in mind run the risk of creating lessons that ignore one or more of the basic needs. Using Figure 10.2 as a reference point, what happens when a teacher provides a lesson with no freedom offered to the students? That depends on both the students and the time of day. If the class is held in the morning, the teacher may get lucky and have a successful lesson with no disruption and high productivity. If there are students in the class with a strong need for freedom, however, even an early-morning class will be problematic. "High-freedom" students will do whatever is necessary to get the freedom they crave. (Remember, all behavior is purposeful.) Since there is no way to satisfy the need for freedom in this lesson by doing what the teacher asks, some students will disrupt the class—even if they do not intend to be disruptive.

If the lesson depicted in Figure 10.2 is offered later in the day, the likelihood of disruption increases exponentially. Especially if they have had very few opportunities to responsibly satisfy their need for freedom throughout the day, students will be more at risk for engaging in inappropriate behavior. Everywhere I travel, teachers tell me that there are more disruptions and office referrals later in the day than in the morning. That is because too many teachers create lessons that don't allow students to get the freedom they need responsibly. By the afternoon, many students are so driven by the unmet need for freedom that disruption is rampant.

How can a teacher be proactive and use the information Figure 10.2 provides? When I ask this question in workshops, teachers quickly come up with simple solutions to infuse freedom into this lesson. Some ideas are

- Morning work/problem of the day—Offer the students a choice of two problems.

- Review homework—Let students "pass" once during the review.
- Quiz—On a 10-question quiz, have students choose any five questions. Or require students to answer the first three questions because they cover the most essential concepts, and allow them to choose any other two questions.

It's not important that you implement *all* of these suggestions. For example, if you think it's crucial that every student answer every question on the quiz, then don't offer choice on the quiz. Determine where you can provide choice without compromising your teaching objective. What is essential is that students are given the opportunity to have freedom and make choices within your classroom. If they are not given those opportunities, you invite trouble and less productivity into your classroom.

Figure 10.2 illustrates a proposed lesson that lacks freedom. Sometimes you will discover that what you are considering doesn't give students a chance to connect with each other and satisfy the drive to belong. Other times, you may have a number of valid activities on the agenda but no activities planned in which students can have fun and enjoy themselves. By tweaking your plans, you can save your lesson from being ravaged by disruption and create a classroom that will be engaging for all students.

Summary

I have shared the concept of planning with the students' needs in mind with thousands of teachers. When they see how little time it takes and the considerable benefits of the process, many are eager to incorporate it into their daily lesson planning. The feedback I have received confirms that this is a simple, time-efficient way to ensure that your lessons will be need-satisfying for your students. Combined with effective instructional strategies and clearly identified learning objectives, planning with students' needs in mind will reduce disruption in your classroom and enhance your effectiveness as a teacher.

Getting Started

- Make sure to consider the basic needs of your students when you create your lesson plans. Even if your plans are well designed and have valid learning objectives, you will succeed only by making sure the class is a need-satisfying experience for the students.

- Use any of the following to help students satisfy the need for belonging and connecting:

  — Assign each student in the classroom a learning partner. Throughout your lesson, ask the students to discuss what they have been learning with their partner. This keeps the conversations on task while helping students meet the need for belonging. Think-Pair-Share experiences also provide students with time to process new learning, a practice that deepens understanding.

  — Rotate routine class responsibilities, such as passing out materials, collecting assignments, and erasing the board. By making sure that every student has a chance to participate in these activities, you will create a classroom community where every student participates and is a contributing member of the class.

  — When appropriate, allow students to work in pairs on a quiz or assignment. Students need to be prepared to defend their work, but only one paper is turned in. This allows students to meet their need for belonging, helps them develop important collaborative skills, and reduces the amount of correcting you have to do.

  — When reviewing for a test, have students work in teams. After asking a question, allow team members to work together on their answer. Not only will they enjoy the social experience, but students frequently learn more easily from their peers because they "speak the same language."

- Use any of the following to help students satisfy their need for freedom and autonomy:

— Give as many choices as possible without sacrificing your authority or compromising the educational objective. The more choices students have, the more easily they accept it when they are told certain things must be done.

— When giving an assignment, allow students to construct an alternative, as long as what they develop addresses the same objectives as your assignment. (Note: When students know they can *always* create an alternative assignment, they seldom do, but they feel considerably less "controlled" and appreciate the freedom they experience.)

— Not everything we teach is essential. When creating tests, require students to answer all the "essential" questions, but give them some choice regarding other questions. For example, students may be required to answer questions 1, 2, and 3, along with any two of the remaining five questions on a test.

— Most teachers give their students numerous choices throughout the day. Make sure your students are consciously aware of the options you provide. This will be especially helpful when you announce that something *must* be done. Students who believe that they have adequate freedom will be compliant. Students who have just as much freedom but aren't as aware of it are more likely to defy even the most reasonable requests.

• Use any of the following to help students satisfy their need for fun:

— Remember that there is a strong connection between fun and learning. When you create an environment that includes fun, you are supporting high achievement. Make your classroom a joyful environment.

— Students of all ages enjoy games and friendly competition. Fun does not have to be purposeless. When it's time to review, use a game format to engage the students and keep the class enjoyable. This keeps the class productive while infusing fun into the experience.

—Take your subject seriously, but never forget that you are working with children. It's perfectly OK to enjoy yourself! The most productive work environments are those that are enjoyable. The same applies in the classroom.

—Remember that part of the fun of learning is making new connections and discoveries. A fun-filled classroom is one that offers reasonable challenges so that students of varying abilities can make new discoveries.

• Follow the process outlined in this chapter for a two-week period. If you are like other teachers, you will find that your lesson planning will improve when you plan with the students' needs in mind. Once you discover this for yourself, you'll want to make this simple strategy a part of your daily planning process.

Teach Your Students to Consciously Self-Evaluate

One of the amazing natural functions of the human brain is to continually compare what we want against what we perceive. Because we are inundated with so much information, most of this internal comparison occurs automatically, out of our awareness. There are times, however, when it is advantageous to be conscious of this process, intentionally evaluate the effectiveness of our actions, and plan accordingly. This is particularly true when it comes to making decisions regarding our education.

Too many students go through school blissfully unaware of their academic goals. As a result, they are less likely to make the kind of academic progress we want them to make. Students who are conscious of what they want (their academic goals) are significantly more aware of how effectively they are working toward those goals. Instead of having this task occur nonconsciously, overseen by a brain primarily concerned with safety and survival, conscious self-evaluation allows us to focus more fully on the behaviors that will increase our competence through academic achievement.

This chapter focuses on how a skillful teacher helps her students develop their internal pictures of a quality writing assignment and use rubrics to self-evaluate their work.

Teaching Students to Self-Evaluate

We all self-evaluate. Constantly. Consciously or nonconsciously, we compare our perception of the reality we want with the reality we perceive at that moment. This internal evaluation drives us to either maintain our current behavior or change it so we have a better chance of getting what we want.

The fact that we are wired to self-evaluate does not mean that we do it consciously or well. The quality of our self-evaluation is dependent upon both the clarity of our wants and the accuracy of our perception of reality. Good teachers help their students become significantly more effective self-evaluators, something that has both academic and social benefits.

Let's begin by considering the internal pictures or wants that are the source of all motivation. It is not unusual for students to lack clarity about what it is that they want in school. Teachers frequently ignore this important concept and naively assume that their students want what the teacher wants: academic success. Just because you have created a lesson with well-defined learning objectives and you know exactly what you want the students to learn and be able to do when it is over, it is foolhardy to assume that all of the students who walk into your classroom want the same thing. In truth, most students have only vaguely defined pictures of what they want from an academic experience. They may want to "do well," or "be successful," or "learn a lot," but most would be hard-pressed to explain exactly what they mean. Students driven by the vaguest of pictures cannot summon the same high level of motivation as those who have a more clearly defined idea of what they want. For that reason, it is essential to develop clarity and a shared perception about what "being successful" means.

Ms. Guerekis

A look into Krista Guerekis's classroom reveals an effective teacher helping her students develop a clear picture of what they want before beginning a writing assignment in her English class.

"OK, guys," she began. "It's time to shift gears and get ready to start our writing project. As your teacher, I want you to be successful. I need you to take a few moments and do some writing in your journal. Specifically, I'm asking you to consider the following questions: Do *you* want to be successful on this assignment? What does 'successful' mean to you? Imagine achieving the kind of success you want. How will you feel? Do you want to experience that feeling? Do you know what you need to do, and are you willing to put in the effort needed to achieve your goal?" Ms. Guerekis moved to the front of the room and revealed a piece of chart paper with the writing prompts she had just provided orally to the students.

"I hope you'll think seriously about these questions as you write. This is *your* education, and I want you to be as clear as possible about what you want to learn and how you define 'success.' After you've finished your journal entry, you may take out something to read silently until everyone has finished. Then we'll have some conversation to see if we have the kind of shared vision we need. You may begin." I watched as the students took out their journals and began to write. Krista and I used the independent student work time to discuss her approach.

"In most classrooms I visit," I began, "teachers give the assignment and tell the students that they expect them to do their best work. Instead of telling, you asked the students to write about the success they want and what 'successful' means to them. Why the different approach?"

"Taking a few minutes to have the kids reflect allows them to develop clear pictures of what *they* want to achieve, which translates into increased motivation and better writing," Krista answered. "If I weren't convinced this process leads directly to better writing, I wouldn't waste our time."

"Tell me how it works," I said.

"People are motivated from inside by what they want," Krista explained. "If I tell the students what *I* want, that's OK, but it doesn't mean for a minute that it matches what they want. You may have noticed that I began the class by telling the students that I want them to be successful. My want is not irrelevant, especially if I develop a strong relationship with my students and they respect me. But a good connection with the kids is still only part of the equation. By having the students reflect and write in their journals, I'm giving them the chance to articulate for themselves that they want to be successful. It helps them take responsibility for their learning. I want them to acknowledge to themselves that being successful feels good and is something *they* want, not simply something their teacher wants or something they do to please someone like their parents. Once the kids *own it* and clarify what they want, they are much more likely to bring to the assignment the kind of drive and motivation needed to do the highest-quality work."

"What about the other questions you asked? Tell me about their purpose, if you will."

"Sure," said Krista. "First, I want the kids to define success for themselves. I've been doing this for quite some time, and I'm convinced that kids impose much higher standards upon themselves than we do, as long as they have ownership over the process."

"Explain that a little bit for me," I said.

"When we provide the standards to the students—the usual practice—they may or may not accept our standards. In fact, sometimes they defy us simply because the standards were externally imposed. When I ask the kids to define what success means to them, it invites them into the process of education. I'm creating a partnership with my students. I'm asking them to take an active role in their own education and take responsibility for their own learning. When I do that, they tend to set standards that are both challenging and reasonable. 'Challenging,' because kids want to achieve, and there can be no feeling of achievement without a sufficient challenge. 'Reasonable,' because kids want to succeed, and creating an unrealistic challenge foils their attempt."

"Is it really that simple?" I asked.

"Of course not!" Krista exclaimed with a laugh. "The less glamorous grunt work that makes it succeed takes place behind the scenes beforehand."

"And what does that involve?" I queried.

"None of this works without a strong, trusting relationship with my students. I need to establish my credibility with them. They need to know my role as their teacher. They have to trust that I'm there to help them and that this is a class where it is safe to take risks and fail. If I didn't do all of that—what I called 'grunt work' a moment ago—then we wouldn't have the environment necessary for helpful self-evaluation. Goal setting and self-evaluation involve risk taking. If students don't trust that I'm their ally, they will set easily attained but paltry goals, so that they won't fail and risk being criticized by me. If I want them to stretch themselves, set high standards, and be willing to fail from time to time, I need to create a positive relationship with my students—one built on trust."

"Talk to me about the questions related to visualizing success and how success feels," I encouraged.

"I want the kids to get the clearest picture of success and have the highest level of motivation. Everybody wants to feel good. Having the students imagine they have been successful and feel good about themselves increases the chances that they will sustain their motivation throughout an extended writing project. The same is true for any long-term assignment where sustained effort is necessary to be successful. Throughout the unit, I'll come back to this concept with some frequency, asking the students to imagine they have completed the assignment in a successful way. I want them to stay connected to the positive feeling that hard work brings. Especially on a major writing assignment with multiple drafts and considerable editing, students need to sustain their motivation if they are to be successful. Visualization and recognition of the positive feelings that come with hard work and success helps them hang in there when it's tempting to give up. I want my students to remain focused on their academic goals and not get discouraged during the predictable moments when things are difficult. Success is the result of hard work and sustained effort. Part of my job is to help kids sustain their motivation when it would be so easy to give up. Goal setting, visualization, and self-evaluation all contribute to that process."

At this point, the students had finished writing in their journals, and the class engaged in a brief discussion about their goals for the upcoming unit. What impressed me most about the discussion was that the students displayed genuine energy and excitement about the upcoming assignment. I have sat in too many classrooms where students said the "right" things but seemed to lack the enthusiasm that Krista's students exhibited.

Helping students develop a clear picture of what they want does not guarantee their success. A well-defined want represents only one-half of the self-evaluation process. The other half involves our perception of reality. At this point, students in Krista's classroom knew what they wanted. In order to self-evaluate effectively as they worked through the writing assignment, they needed to have accurate perceptions of their work. Krista helped her students do this as well, so that they wouldn't self-evaluate with inaccurate or incomplete perceptions.

"I'm delighted that you all have a clear picture of success for yourselves," Krista told the class as she prepared to move to the next phase of the lesson. "After hearing your comments, I'm comfortable that we have a shared vision. You and I want the same thing, and that will make it easier for us to work well together. But simply having a picture of what you want isn't enough," she went on. "You need to know if you are on the right track. This should help." Krista then distributed a four-page packet to each student. "What I've given you are four separate excerpts from projects that were done by former students. I've labeled the samples A, B, C, and D. One of the samples would earn a 1 on our rubric. One would earn a 2. One would earn a 3. And one would earn a 4. Your job is to read the samples and grade each one. You can work in groups of two or three students, and we'll discuss your answers as a class. In addition to assigning a grade to each paper, you need to explain why you gave a particular grade. What did the paper have—or lack—that led you to grade it as you did? Any questions?" As there were none, Krista told her students to begin.

"Will you explain this part to me?" I asked her, as the students immersed themselves in their task.

"During the first activity," replied Krista, "the students created a picture of what they wanted. This is a writing assignment that will include multiple drafts. Throughout the process, I'll want them to regularly assess their progress so they can attain their goals. If I simply have them work without providing adequate guidance and support, many of the papers they turn in will not be particularly well written. Even though it's easy to self-evaluate, the quality of our self-evaluation is directly connected to the quality of our perceptions and available information. Without models or a rubric, I would end up with a batch of papers that are unnecessarily substandard. This exercise will give us a common perception of what a paper looks like that merits a 1, 2, 3, or 4 on the rubric we use in our class."

"So this helps them self-evaluate more accurately?" I asked.

"Exactly," she answered. "Asking kids to assess their work without giving them a model or rubric is patently unfair. As the teacher, I'm ultimately responsible for issuing a grade. If I want them to fully engage in the process, I need to find ways for them to get information easily and accurately. I think you'll enjoy the conversation we'll have as a class in a few minutes."

Krista was right. The students found it fairly easy to identify the sample that deserved a 4 for work that was outstanding and above grade-level expectations. It was equally easy for them to identify the deficient, highly flawed 1. Determining what was a 2 and what was a 3 was more of a challenge, since both samples had flaws and both had merit. Through skillful questioning, Krista was able to help the students discover what characteristics were most important in creating a competent piece of writing. By the end of the discussion, each student agreed which paper was a 2 and which was a 3, and each could articulate why.

The class was nearly done for the day. Krista Guerekis addressed her students: "As we get ready to begin our initial drafts, I want to ask you a few questions. First, give me a thumbs-up if you have a picture of success, something that will leave you feeling good about yourself and your accomplishments when you're done." Every student gave a thumbs-up. "Just as importantly, are you leaving here today with a clear idea about what you need to show me to achieve the success you want?" Again, every student offered a thumbs-up. "Great! Tonight I want you to prepare your initial draft. Use the models I gave you and the notes you took during our discussion to create a piece that will get you on the road to where you want to be."

Commentary

Teaching students how to consciously self-evaluate is essential if we want the majority of our students to regularly engage in the highest-quality work. As Krista Guerekis demonstrated, it's crucial to have students develop clarity about what they want in order to evaluate effectively. The development of a strong "want" provides the motivation students need to sustain their effort over time. By providing students with clear models and rubrics, we ensure that their perceptions are grounded in accurate knowledge when they assess their work.

In addition to teaching students to self-evaluate regarding their academic performance, we can teach students to be more intentional about their social behavior. During my career as a school psychologist and administrator, I frequently asked students to identify the kind of young man or young woman they wanted to be. As they consciously built a picture of the kind of person they wanted to be (and become), they were more likely to engage in the prosocial, positive behaviors we value in school. As a classroom teacher, Krista asked her students to look at sample papers to help them develop accurate perceptions about academic performance. Working in a non-classroom role, I would ask students questions like the following: "You said you would like to be a 'good' person. If you were a 'good' person, what would you do in this situation?" "If you want to be known as someone who is honest, what do you think you should do?" "Forget everyone else for a moment. Pretend no one will ever know what you do. What decision will help you feel good about yourself?" Questions like these help learners of all ages create powerful internal motivation and inspire strong character in our students.

As we evaluate ourselves and others, we are limited by the accuracy of the knowledge we possess. That's why rubrics are essential. They provide us with well-defined measures of what quality looks like. Krista Guerekis used a rubric to help her students identify what 1, 2, 3, and 4 papers looked like. I have been in classrooms where teachers have posted rubrics on the walls and asked students to check their efforts against the rubric before turning them in. I have watched students who thought they were done consult the rubric and return to their seats to make changes to their work rather than turn in a low-quality paper to the teacher. Having rubrics on the wall is a useful strategy for several reasons. First, as part of the visual environment, they contribute to the nonconscious learning that goes on in every classroom. In addition, requiring students to get up and move to check their papers introduces movement in the classroom, something that is especially helpful for students who require movement.

When we teach students to self-evaluate with intentionality, they develop responsibility. In too many classrooms, students engage in slovenly work and rely on their teacher to fix their errors. Students who self-evaluate and make use of carefully created rubrics and other models of quality are more likely to produce better work. This supports higher achievement.

Finally, asking students to self-evaluate and take greater responsibility saves the teacher valuable time while fostering higher-quality work. When I taught English, our curriculum coordinator determined that the students needed to write more. I was already overwhelmed by the amount of reading and correcting I needed to do with 125 students. To accommodate the district mandate to have the students write more while simultaneously keeping myself from being overwhelmed by increased correcting, I devised a folder system with my students. I told them that each week, they were to put a final draft in their folder. Once a paper was placed in the folder, it meant the student had evaluated the assignment and was ready to have it graded by me. I told them that I would not evaluate each paper but would choose some randomly. To ensure that I read their best work, near the end of each marking period I asked the students to evaluate their papers and indicate the two they wanted me to read. Beyond that, I informed the students, I would read two or three additional papers each marking period. In all, I ended up reading only about half of what they wrote, something that saved me considerable time. Because the students knew that anything in the folder might be read and graded, they carefully self-evaluated to make sure their work represented their best writing. And because I allowed them to choose two of the papers that would be read and graded, there were no complaints that the system was unfair. By teaching my students to self-evaluate and take more responsibility for their learning, they did better work, and I was a more successful, more rested, and more satisfied teacher.

Getting Started

- As often as possible, have students identify their picture of quality for each assignment. Be certain to do this with all major assignments. Instead of simply telling students what you expect from them, ask them to articulate what they expect from themselves. Students who create their own pictures of quality will demonstrate increased effort to attain their goals.

- Have your students imagine themselves being successful. Ask them to identify how it *feels* to be academically successful. Visualization of future success, with its attendant positive feelings, helps us sustain motivation when it's easy and tempting to give up. Have students return to their visions of success regularly so that they don't lose sight of their academic goals.

- Provide students with models and rubrics so that they can evaluate their work more accurately. Effective self-evaluation is contingent upon accurate information. Providing students with models and rubrics gives them the necessary tools to self-evaluate in a way that enhances their performance.

- Have students evaluate their work against the models and rubrics you have provided *before* they give it to you for your feedback. This step will result in you correcting assignments that reflect higher-quality work. Having students consult a model or rubric also provides them with an appropriate level of responsibility for their education. Rather than adopting a passive orientation when it comes to evaluation, students become actively involved.

- Teach students to evaluate their behavior as well as their academic performance. Have the students create a vision of a successful class, and ask them to identify the behaviors that would support the kind of class you all want. Ask students questions like the following:
  - "Before we begin today's lesson, think about the behaviors that will help you be a successful student. Will you leave here more satisfied if you behave that way?"
  - "Are you acting like the student/young man/young woman you would like to be?"
  - "What kind of reputation do you want to have? Are you acting in a way that is helping you create the reputation you want?"

Note: It is absolutely essential that you ask students to self-evaluate routinely, *not just when they are having difficulty!* If the only time you ask them to examine their academic performance or classroom behavior is when you are displeased with how they are doing, you are not really asking students to self-evaluate! You are dishonestly using the language of self-evaluation to externally evaluate your students. It is okay for you to externally evaluate your students, but don't confuse it with self-evaluation. Self-evaluation is only effective when it is used in successful situations as well as ones in which students are struggling. Make this practice a part of your standard classroom procedures.

Teach Your Students About the Components of Behavior

Behavior not only consists of an overt, observable action but also includes thoughts, feelings, and a physiological component. These four components of behavior work in concert; therefore, changing any one necessarily affects the other three.

When we are frustrated or angry, it is especially easy to be driven by the feelings component of behavior. Under these conditions, we are prone to engage in behaviors that only exacerbate a difficult situation. Even when things are going well, it is advisable to help children develop behaviors that are more thoughtful and less emotional. A more reflective orientation facilitates academic growth.

From the time they begin school, students can be taught that when they consciously choose to act and think in a positive way, they will automatically feel better and experience an improved physiological state. The result is youngsters who have significantly more effective control over their behavior, as well as ones able to make behavioral choices that will have more pleasant, positive consequences.

This chapter describes how a 2nd grade teacher helps young learners feel good by choosing thoughts and actions that support academic achievement.

Total Behavior

Thanks to the work of William Glasser (1984), we know that behavior includes four components: acting, thinking, feeling, and physiology. I have said before that all behavior is purposeful. We behave in ways that we believe will make us *feel* good. Of the four components of behavior, we are most aware of our feelings and physiology. We know when we are angry, happy, frustrated, excited, or depressed. We know when we are fatigued or energized or have a headache or a stomachache. However, our feelings and physiology are the components of behavior that are most difficult to control or change directly. When you are frustrated, it's hard to stop being frustrated *simply because you want to*. And wouldn't it be nice if you could just decide to get rid of your headache? Unfortunately, as we well know, it's not that easy. But we have considerably more con-trol—albeit indirect control—over our feelings and physiology than most people believe.

We have more immediate control over our actions and thinking. This is important, because the four components of behavior work in concert; when we change any one component of behavior, the other components are affected. So although it's nearly impossible to change how we feel directly, we can have considerable control over how we feel by choosing our actions and thoughts. Some thoughts and actions are congruent with frustration; others automatically lead to a reduc-tion in frustration—or any other unpleasant, unwanted emotion.

Counselors who practice internal control psychology regularly use this concept, which Glasser identified as "total behavior." Coun-selors unfamiliar with internal control psychology often erroneously believe that students will only begin to *do* better when they *feel* bet-ter. While it's true that students will *do* better when they *feel* better, the dilemma is that it's impossible to *feel* better just because we want to! Counselors who are not familiar with total behavior are caught in a catch-22, waiting for underperforming, unhappy students to miraculously *feel* better. This dilemma is solved when we remem-ber that students will *feel* better when they begin to *act* better. By "acting better," I mean acting in a responsible way that helps them get what they want. That is something every student can learn with the help of a skilled teacher or counselor. The result will be happier students who are more likely to accept the academic challenges we offer them.

Counselors who practice internal control psychology typically focus on actions and thoughts, the two components of behavior most easily controlled. With assistance, students can select actions and thoughts that will lead to more positive feelings and a reduction in the somatic complaints that many struggling students experience. Struggling students are easily able to tell you that they feel angry or frustrated or that their stomach hurts. What they don't know is that these feelings and physiological states are directly related to the actions and thoughts they choose. Once they are taught that they will feel better by choosing different, more effective actions and thoughts, the cycle of failure and underperformance can be broken.

Teachers in the classroom can just as easily use the concept of total behavior to enhance academic performance. As the following observation shows, even young children can understand and apply the concept of total behavior to their advantage, and the teacher can use the concept to help students engage in higher-quality academic work.

Mrs. Cronin

Jamilla Cronin had her 23 2nd grade students sitting on the carpet at the front of the classroom. On the board behind her, she had taped a piece of chart paper with a circle divided into four quadrants drawn on it (see Figure 12.1).

"Boys and girls," she began in a soft voice, immediately quieting the children and getting their attention. "As you know, we are starting something new this morning. Today we start learning all about the planets and our solar system. You already know that we live on the planet Earth. Can you name any other planets for me?"

A number of hands shot up, and over the next several minutes Mrs. Cronin conducted an informal assessment of what her 2nd grade students already knew about the solar system. Not surprisingly, their information was limited and often erroneous. Mrs. Cronin discovered fairly quickly that she had a lot of work to do if she hoped to teach her students the concepts that she valued and that are identified in the curriculum frameworks. Mrs. Cronin knew that

Figure 12.1 | Total Behavior Chart

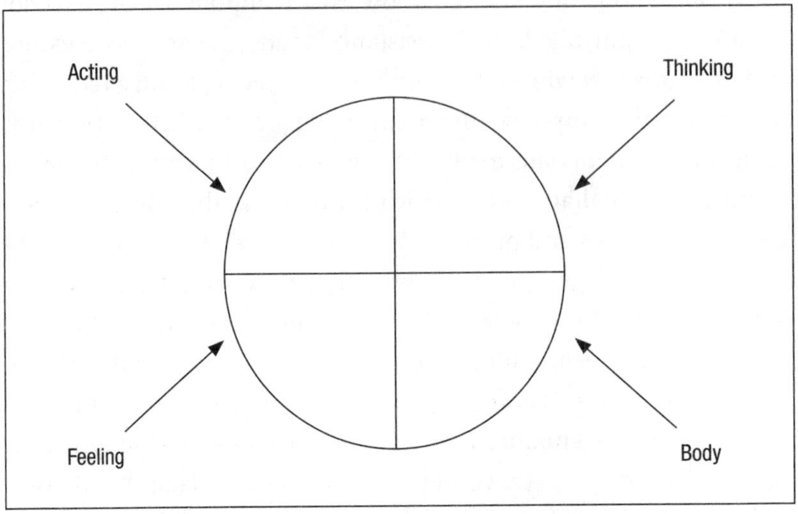

it's easy for youngsters to become frustrated and give up easily, especially in subjects like science. Because she didn't want that to happen to her students, she needed to give them the tools that will help them determine what they need to do to experience the satisfaction that comes with academic success.

"My goodness!" exclaimed Mrs. Cronin at the conclusion of this informal assessment. "There are already so many things you know!" She paused and scanned the room, making eye contact with her students and nodding, acknowledging what they already knew. "And there's so much more I am going to help you learn," she said. "It certainly should be an exciting adventure, don't you think?" The students nodded vigorously.

"Now I want you to look at the chart paper I have taped on the board behind me," the teacher continued. "You can see that I have four words written outside of a circle. Let me ask you something. I want you all to pretend that we've finished studying the solar system. When it's all over, how do you want to feel? Tanya?"

"I want to feel happy, Mrs. Cronin," said Tanya.

"Oh, 'happy,'" echoed Mrs. Cronin. "That's a good one. I like happy. Let me write that in the part of the circle next to 'feelings.' Who else can tell me how they want to feel? Antoine?"

"Me, I want to feel proud of myself," beamed Antoine. As more children offered suggestions of how they wanted to feel, the teacher wrote them on the chart paper.

"Now imagine you were feeling happy, and proud of yourself, and satisfied, and smart," she continued. "How do you think your body would feel?" Mrs. Cronin knew this was a difficult question for 2nd grade students, but she wanted to give them a chance to answer before giving them too many ideas. Experience had taught her that it was better to *ask* as much as possible, teasing out what her students might know, rather than simply *tell*. After a period of silence, she asked, "Do you think you'd have a headache?" As the children laughed, Marcus chimed in, "You don't have a headache when you're happy!"

"Exactly! So how would your body feel?" the teacher asked again.

"I'd just be relaxed, kind of calm," said Sarah.

"Yeah," said Marcus. "Like when I don't do good, I get all messed up inside. Like my stomach hurts, or I get all jittery on the inside. When I'm happy, I'm just chillin'." Mrs. Cronin added the students' comments to the chart paper in the quadrant associated with physiology.

"I think I know how you will answer my next question," she said, "but you know I like to make sure. Do you *want* to be feeling all those nice things we put on the chart paper and have your body feel relaxed and calm?" She once again saw 23 heads nodding in agreement, accompanied by comments like, "You know it."

"I thought so," she said with a smile. "So let's look at the remaining two parts of our circle: acting and thinking. Let's start with 'acting.' Do you think if you don't pay attention in class, that will help?"

"No!" the students bellowed in chorus.

"OK. So give me some suggestions of actions that will help you feel the way you want to feel. What are some things you can *do*?"

"Pay attention," said one student.

"Do your work and don't bother others," added another.

"Ask for help when you don't know what to do," a third student said.

"Make sure you're in school and on time," volunteered another.

Mrs. Cronin wrote down what the children said before moving to the final quadrant: thinking. "When you're doing your work and trying to learn as much as possible about the solar system so you can feel proud of yourself and happy, will 'stinking thinking' help you?" she asked.

Once again, Mrs. Cronin was greeted with a chorus of "No!" from her enthusiastic students. "So tell me what you'd be thinking, even if some of the work is a challenge. I want to know exactly what you'll tell yourselves. Tell me the words that would be in your head."

"I can do this!" said Carlson.

"I know I'm smart enough to figure this out," added Felicia.

"I'm going to feel SO GOOD when I get this!" said Leslie.

"Don't give up! Don't give up!" said Ziggy.

"It's time to look at what we've done," said Mrs. Cronin. The complete chart is shown in Figure 12.2.

"You began by telling me how you want to feel when we're done," the teacher said. "You know we have fun in this class and that we do a lot of work. You're a smart bunch. Tell me how you can feel happy and proud of yourself and all the other positive feelings you want to have. I want you to take out your journals and write 'The keys to success.'" Mrs. Cronin neatly wrote this on the board for the children to copy. "In a moment, it will be time to return to your table, get your journals, and begin. During the time you are writing, you may have a snack. You can write with words or pictures. When everyone is finished, we'll have a little class meeting and discuss what you think are the keys to success. You may quietly return to your tables."

Mrs. Cronin's Teaching Philosophy

I was eager to talk with Jamilla Cronin and learn how she had come to incorporate the concept of total behavior into her classroom instructional strategies.

Figure 12.2 | Mrs. Cronin's Completed Chart

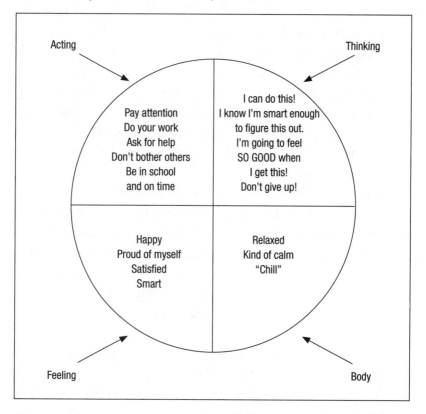

"I know that counselors who practice internal control psychology discuss the relationship among the various components of behavior," I said, "but it's typically not seen in the classroom. What led you to weave this into your teaching?"

"I have a dear friend in another district who is a middle school counselor," Jamilla answered. "As you well know, middle school kids are highly emotional as those hormones begin to rage, and they don't know how to manage things yet. My friend introduced me to the concept of total behavior and recommended some books that gave me a pretty solid understanding of how the four components work together. Even though the idea is used more widely by counselors, it just made sense to me to teach it to my students and use it as a tool to increase academic performance."

"How long have you been using it?" I asked. "And has it been successful?"

"I've been using this for the past few years, and I'm certain it's been very helpful to my students."

"In what ways?" I prodded.

"Well, I have always believed that kids are motivated, but I've been around long enough to know that they aren't always motivated to do what I want them to do and learn what I want them to learn."

"You do realize, " I interrupted, "that some teachers don't believe that all kids are motivated."

Jamilla just smiled. "Oh, yes, I am very aware of that. Let's just say I think they're wrong. It's very convenient to identify kids who don't want to learn what you're trying to teach as 'unmotivated.' It relieves the teacher of any responsibility. I accept that some kids aren't motivated to learn what I'm trying to teach and see it as my job to engage them and spark the desire to learn that all kids have."

"And how does discussing the components of behavior help?" I asked.

"You saw today's class," Jamilla answered. "I begin with the belief that all people want to feel good and be successful. Even though we hear comments like, 'He chose to fail,' I can't for the life of me figure out how or why any person would *choose* to fail. Failure doesn't feel good, and we all want to feel good. That's why I begin my conversation with the students by asking them how they want to *feel* when we finish studying something."

"Do you always begin with feelings?" I asked.

"I do," answered Jamilla. "It makes good sense to start where people want to be—feeling good—and move from there. Plus, as the students imagine feeling good, they get more engaged and animated. Did you see the students become more excited when they talked about feeling proud of themselves and things like that?" Jamilla asked.

"I did notice that."

"In the old days, before I started doing this," Jamilla continued, "I would simply introduce the lesson. Some kids would be motivated and excited because the topic appealed to them. Some would be engaged because they wanted to please me. That's fairly common among 2nd grade students. But there were always a few who didn't much care about the topic and weren't especially interested in pleasing the teacher."

"How does this approach engage those kids?" I asked.

"By going directly to the good feelings all students want to experience—that becomes their reward. It's not about pleasing me or their parents or getting some ticket they can redeem at the school store. It's about feeling good, being proud of themselves, and experiencing the joy that comes with developing a work ethic, something too many students lack today. Once the students connect positive academic behaviors with feeling good, things fall into place pretty easily."

"You make it sound almost magical," I said. "Are there no reluctant learners?"

"Of course there are!" Jamilla said with a laugh. "I'm good, but I'm not a magician. I still face a range of abilities. I have kids with tremendous support from home and others with virtually none. There are still challenges, but I know my students put forth much greater effort now and achieve much more than they did before I began emphasizing the components of behavior. Even reluctant learners are more engaged when they see that they can feel better by choosing thoughts and actions that support learning."

"Let me play devil's advocate for a moment," I said. "There are many people who think that kids, especially in elementary school, are too young to be as future-oriented as you are asking them to be. Youngsters live in the present, and you're asking them to think about the end of a unit of study. What do you say to those who question if young children are developmentally ready to take on the responsibility you're asking them to take on?"

"I agree that youngsters are impulsive and live in the present. I'm not naive. Why do you think I put things on chart paper instead of the board? So we can keep it and refer to it. It keeps it in the present. I regularly refer to our chart and help kids stay focused on what they can do *now*—present tense—to help them achieve what they want. Plus, I sometimes get frustrated with people who talk about kids being too impulsive and stuck in the present."

"Tell me more," I said.

"It's one of those convenient truths that allows adults to abdicate responsibility. Yes, kids are impulsive. Yes, kids are not skilled at delaying gratification. Yes, kids have difficulty creating long-term goals and sustaining effort to achieve what they want. So isn't it my job to help them grow in those areas? I'm a teacher. It's my job to help kids develop those capacities. Complaining about what students *can't* do is not something that helps me feel better. For me to experience the positive feelings I want, it's more helpful to teach my students how to develop greater control. Teaching them about the components of behavior gets me where I want to go. Expecting that kids are magically going to develop the capacity to be future-minded and mature is foolish. Kids need our guidance and support to mature. Young kids need it more than anyone. I think what I do helps kids mature and take responsibility for their learning, as well as decreasing—but not eliminating—their impulsivity and fostering the academic mind-set we want." Jamilla paused and looked at me. "OK. End of sermon. Time to get off my soapbox."

"Please," I said. "I asked for your feedback and comments. Is there anything else you'd like to add?"

"In that case," Jamilla continued with a hearty laugh, "I do have one other point. I believe fervently in responsibility. And I mean taking responsibility for the good as well as the bad. Lots of people use the term *responsibility* like it's bad. In my head, it's just about taking ownership of our lives. A lot of children in elementary school do pretty well. In many cases, the strong relationship between the teacher and the students supports their achievement, but too many kids think they do well because they were 'lucky' or the tasks were 'easy.' And the few who do poorly are quick to say things like, 'The teacher doesn't like me' or 'The test was hard.' I want my students to see that their success and their struggles are the result of what they choose to do. I want to help them develop a sense of responsibility and ownership for their lives. I don't want them to think they feel good because they got 'lucky.' Absolutely not. I want them to *know* they feel good because of the actions they took and the thinking they did. Teaching my kids about the four components of behavior and how our acting and thinking impact our feeling and physiology helps them grow into the responsible students I want them to become."

I thanked Jamilla Cronin, profoundly impressed by this passionate teacher who does so much to help her students appreciate that they have much more control of their lives than they might otherwise believe.

Summary

The concept of total behavior is powerful. Because all people are motivated to feel good, educators can teach the components of behavior to students so they can develop more effective control over their behavior and act in ways that enhance their academic growth. Jamilla Cronin made her 2nd grade students aware that the actions they take and the thoughts they choose have a direct impact on their feelings and somatic state. The fact that even young learners can appreciate these connections suggests that we can create classrooms where students want to act more responsibly and exercise greater control over their lives. While counselors using internal control psychology have taught their counselees about the components of behavior for a long time, Jamilla demonstrates how classroom teachers can use this powerful concept to their advantage as they deliver instruction to students and seek to engage them in their own educational journey.

Getting Started

- Directly teach your students about the four components of behavior: acting, thinking, feeling, and physiology. In addition to identifying the components of behavior, help students discover that changing one component affects them all. You can use a simple example like the one that follows to quickly teach this complex concept:

    Ask the students to pretend they play basketball (or any other sport you think they enjoy). They have just had a game in which they played poorly and their team lost. Ask them how they feel and what thoughts are going through their head. Ask them to identify their physiological state, but don't worry if the students struggle with this component of behavior. Then ask the students how they would like to feel. Discuss what actions and thoughts have the best chance of helping them experience the positive feelings they want. Once you have walked the students through this simple, nonacademic situation, you can move into a discussion about the components of behavior as they relate to an upcoming assignment.

- Ask (don't *tell*) your students how they want to feel about themselves in school. Even struggling, underperforming students want to feel good about themselves. When they learn the concept of total behavior, students will see that they can act and think in specific ways to achieve the feelings they want.
- Once students identify that they want to feel successful and proud of themselves, teach them that they have the greatest chance of getting what they want if they choose their actions and thoughts carefully. Feelings are important. They act as signals, informing us if our behaviors are effective or not. But it's best to concentrate on the acting and thinking components of behavior, because these are the components we can most easily control directly. Students driven by emotion are more volatile and erratic, often engaging in behavior that is counterproductive. Teach your students to adopt a more reflective approach by concentrating on the thoughts and actions that will lead to the positive feelings they desire.
- Emphasize the concept of total behavior when students have done well. One especially effective practice is to discuss total behavior after your students have had success. You know they feel good. Have them identify what they did and the thoughts they engaged in. Then ask them if they want to experience the same feeling of satisfaction again. They will soon learn that they have considerable control over how they feel when they decide what to do and how to think. When students make that

discovery, they take much greater responsibility for their education because they know they are very much in control of their lives. Help your students take responsibility for their success as well as for their shortcomings.

Teach Less, Teach Deeply

In virtually every subject area, the curriculum is expanding, which means that teachers are expected to cover more, and students are expected to digest more. Our obsession with a "more is better" mentality has led to a supersized curriculum that necessitates a superficial approach to teaching. For students to make greater academic progress, they must be given adequate time to study fewer concepts. Deep learning requires time to process new information so that students move beyond surface knowledge and develop the competence to apply what they have learned. Today's bloated curriculum provides too little time for processing, as teachers and students work at a frenetic pace in an effort to "cover" the required material. It doesn't have to be this way.

Using state standards and the principles of standards-based education, teachers can downsize the curriculum to facilitate deeper learning. This requires us to thoroughly examine course content and make decisions about what concepts are most essential and deserving of the time and energy needed for meaningful learning to occur. If we abandon a broad, ill-defined curriculum and create one that is more narrowly focused, we will provide teachers and students an essential resource: adequate time for learning.

This chapter examines how to better use existing resources, such as state standards and the ideas of standards-based education, to be more selective about what we teach and to deliver instruction that will result in a deeper understanding of essential concepts.

Narrowing Our Focus

When my children were young, we took a family vacation to the Southwest for a couple of weeks. It was wonderful to see East Coast kids getting their first glimpse of a completely different terrain, highlighted by the majesty of the Grand Canyon. We all agreed, however, that we spent too much time in the car, skimming the surface and in transition, and not enough time "doing it." Years later, what our kids remember most (and most fondly) about that trip was an afternoon spent at Goblin State Park in Utah, where we took time to run around, playing hide-and-seek amid formations that were completely alien to us, and the days we spent at Zion National Park in Utah, because we had the good sense to stay several nights in one place and got to know the park pretty well. No one talks about Arches National Park, where we drove in, took a brief walk and a few great pictures, and quickly returned to the car. And no one even remembers going to Canyon National Park, although I have some receipts that prove we were there, however briefly. When my son, now in his mid-20s, recently found out that my wife and I were planning a return trip to Zion National Park, he said, "Let me know when you're going. I'll see if I can get a few days off and join you. That was an incredible place. I'd like to go back there."

What does this have to do with education? Today, more than ever before, we try to cover too much ground in too little time. The result is an unnecessarily superficial approach to teaching and learning. Even if the experience is pleasant enough in the moment—as most of our family's Southwest experiences were—we need depth and time for lasting memories to form and significant learning to occur. Throughout this book, I have trumpeted the importance of developing positive relationships with students, but positive relationships alone don't guarantee a quality educational experience. Positive relationships pave the way, but we need ample time to move beyond a shallow approach to learning.

In *Results Now,* Mike Schmoker (2006) makes a compelling argument that we teach far too much today, choosing breadth over depth.

He suggests that our students would benefit if we become more selective about what we teach and plunge more deeply into those things that we identify as worthy of study. Throughout his book, Schmoker provides persuasive evidence in support of the notion that teaching less and teaching deeply will lead to significant academic gains in a very short time. The research he cites is impressive.

Although Schmoker makes a compelling case for fewer course offerings, I am not advocating a bare-bones curriculum that eliminates art, music, physical education, foreign language, and other courses beyond English, math, science, and social studies. To prepare our students for a successful adult life in an increasingly interdependent world, exposure to the arts is essential. Furthermore, numerous studies suggest that students who pursue courses in physical education and the arts fare better in traditional academic classes as well (Jensen, 1998). When I suggest narrowing what we teach, I am referring to what we choose to teach in any given course. An expansive offering of courses helps students develop into well-rounded adults with a less egocentric perspective of the world. Within each course experience, however, we need to be highly selective about what we teach, giving a limited number of topics adequate time for meaningful learning.

Everywhere I go, teachers complain that the already bloated curriculum in their subject area continues to expand. What is the result of demanding more from teachers? When we require teachers to cover more content, we sacrifice quality. Remember that we have an innate drive for freedom. Increased curricular requirements, especially requirements that teachers don't wholeheartedly endorse, are naturally met with resistance. The result is teachers who comply with the mandate to cover more but do so grudgingly, without the energy and commitment needed to inspire their students in large numbers.

Under increased pressure to cover more, teachers are stressed, less patient with their students, and forced to take a more hurried, perfunctory approach that continually leaves behind marginal students. The more hurried teachers are, the more unavailable they are to struggling students who need a little extra time and attention to master difficult concepts. What makes our preoccupation with supersizing the curriculum especially puzzling and misguided is how disconnected it is from what employers want from us. Consider the following excerpt from *Leadership That Reaches Every Student* (Graham, 2007):

> *Educational Leadership* (April 2007) ranks the skills that employers will look for in their employees over the next five years as (1) critical thinking/problem solving, (2) information technology, (3) teamwork/collaboration, (4) creativity/innovation, (5) diversity, and (6) leadership (Levine, 2007). According to the study, mathematics, writing, foreign language, and reading comprehension were ranked toward the bottom. (p. xv)

One of our professional responsibilities is to prepare students to be productive employees in the future. Paradoxically, our current fascination with building a bigger curriculum compromises our teachers' ability to equip students with the skills they will need to be successful in the world of work. If we were to offer a streamlined academic experience, teachers would have time to teach more deeply and incorporate the collaborative "people skills" that will help students succeed later in life.

Teachers aren't the only ones who suffer under and resent a curriculum that demands too much and provides inadequate time for deep learning; students are victimized in multiple ways. First, because the pace of the class is so hurried, the student–teacher relationship is compromised. Students who lack a positive connection with their teacher find it much easier to disrupt class during instructional time, meeting their social need inappropriately. A positive connection with a teacher serves as an essential segue for those students who are not already excited about the course content. Stripped of that positive connection, many students who *could* become excited about learning remain uninvolved and aloof.

Even engaged students who value what is being taught and want to do well are hurt by a curriculum that sacrifices quality for quantity. Effective learning includes two complementary psychological states: paying attention and making meaning. When teachers provide information through direct instruction, textbooks, or other sources of input, students need to pay attention to the incoming information. But this external orientation, while a necessary component in the learning process, can only take us so far. Learning that is based exclusively on paying attention is superficial and low-level, because students have not been given the opportunity to reflect, make meaning, and engage in the process of internalization necessary for deeper learning. Superficial learning is adequate when our goal is to prepare students to learn simple facts and answer true/false or multiple-choice questions. When we want students to synthesize concepts and apply what they have learned, however, they need time to internalize and "own" the information. They need time to make meaning. A curriculum that has students moving frenetically from concept to concept denies them the time to internalize and make meaning of what has been taught.

Finally, the human brain is designed to assess the constant input with which we are bombarded and identify what is important and what is less relevant. We naturally strive to prioritize incoming information. The overstuffed curriculum short-circuits this natural tendency by reducing everything to equal importance. A teacher may introduce a new concept to students, cautioning, "This is important. Pay close attention." But before students can fully assimilate the new information, the teacher races to the next topic, repeating the increasingly meaningless mantra, "This is important. Pay close attention." Overwhelmed, students' brains adopt a coping strategy designed to keep them from being swamped by less important information. In an attempt to prioritize, the brain decides, "This probably isn't important. We've heard this before and moved on before we even scratched the surface. Don't pay too much attention to this." What makes this reaction so difficult to combat is the fact that it occurs outside conscious awareness.

How Do We Choose?

Faced with an oversized curriculum, how does a teacher choose what to emphasize? No teacher wants to eliminate topics and content that may be especially important, unintentionally doing students a disservice. With virtually every state having adopted standards and curriculum frameworks, teachers have easy access to a guide that will help them identify those aspects of their curriculum that require their time and attention.

While it's a good first step, using the state standards as a guide won't be enough if you want to teach less and teach deeply. You may scale down somewhat, but the state standards remain too massive to be taught deeply and effectively to all students in the time allotted. While a few academically talented students can manage the demands of an extensive curriculum, the majority of our students will be over-whelmed and resort to learning strategies designed to successfully negotiate the demands of a class even though their learning is little more than superficial. Fortunately, standards-based education (SBE) provides a model that can help. In SBE, concepts are identified as "essential to know," "important to know," and "nice to know." See the visual representation of the concept in Figure 13.1.

Using the SBE model, teachers can determine what parts of the curriculum are essential, important, and nice to know. It is crucial that educators be discriminating in what they teach, especially in

Figure 13.1 | Standards-Based Education Model

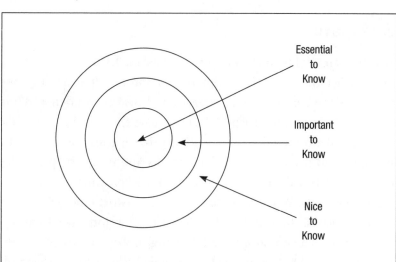

today's world, where the sheer vastness of available information is overwhelming. Those aspects teachers identify as "essential" should form the core of their instruction. These are the concepts that require the most instructional time and that they should endeavor to teach most deeply. Those elements they identify as "important" deserve some attention but not nearly as much as the "essential" content and skills. The remaining aspects, those things that are "nice to know," can be introduced to competent students as enrichment work or opportunities for students to extend their learning. Devoting precious class time and direct instruction to these elements, however, compromises a teacher's ability to emphasize what is truly essential and important.

A word of caution: It would not be prudent for any teacher to make important curricular decisions in isolation. A district should make a collaborative choice about what to focus on in an effort to teach less and teach deeply. Teachers who make curricular decisions unilaterally leave themselves open to criticism and administrative action. While I strongly advocate that we teach less and teach deeply, I would never want to see a teacher hurt because he or she acted in good faith but independently. Maverick teachers acting alone put themselves at risk and do little more than return us to the days when the curriculum lacked prudent, meaningful uniformity.

Summary

Teachers are right—they are currently asked to teach too much. The predictable result is a superficial approach to teaching, one that lacks the substance that engages and inspires students. While individual classroom teachers lack great authority, they can take steps to streamline what they teach so that learning is deeper. By making good use of the state frameworks and using the principles of standards-based education, classroom teachers can take small but significant steps. When an entire school or district engages in these same strategies, the results will be even more impressive. I encourage every teacher to adopt the following motto: "I will cover less, teach more, and help students learn deeply." When course demands are streamlined and students are provided with the time necessary to learn deeply, more students will be more engaged and make greater academic progress.

Getting Started

- Examine your curriculum and identify what is "essential to know," what is "important to know," and what is "nice to know." Effective teaching requires us to discriminate and prioritize.
- Make a commitment to focus your instruction on those things that are "essential" and "important." As easy as this sounds, this step may require you to give up teaching some things that you especially enjoy. Most teachers find that they dedicate considerable instructional time to concepts that are nonessential simply because those concepts are some of their favorites.
- Be judicious in how you spend time, making certain that this most precious resource is wisely allocated. Because time is such a valuable commodity, make a commitment to highlight those essential concepts that will best serve your students over time. As your students perform better and learn more deeply, you will find that your need for competence is better satisfied.
- Don't act in isolation! Be certain that you have administrative support when you decide to teach fewer concepts more deeply. The best strategy is for a school or district to make decisions collaboratively. The process of carefully reviewing the curriculum and determining what is most essential helps teachers develop increased energy and passion for the streamlined, common curriculum. This leads to more inspired teaching that results in enhanced student performance.
- Regardless of what you teach, provide students with ample time to reflect and make meaning of what they are being asked to learn. Structure your lessons so that students have time to reflect. Give them opportunities to personalize the learning by asking them to relate what they are learning to their own lives. Finally, ask students to demonstrate that they can apply what you have taught. Unless students are given adequate

time, they will be unable to apply what they have learned, and their education will remain woefully inadequate and superficial. Make sure that everything you deem important enough to teach is given enough time for meaningful reflection and deep learning.

14

Create Your Professional Identity

Throughout this book, the focus has been on students. It's time to turn our attention to you, the educator. You will benefit from determining the kind of educator you want to be and the kind of contribution you want to make to the profession you have chosen. Even though you are part of a large "system," it's important to be more than just another cog on the wheel. Creating a strong, unique professional identity and professional goals will help you satisfy your innate drive to be powerful and competent. Meeting the expectations of others may be necessary, but defining and meeting your own expectations are equally essential if you hope to have a satisfying professional experience.

To become an effective teacher and inspire your students, you need to create your own professional identity and mission statement. This chapter will guide you through a process that will help you become the educator you want to be. Active engagement in this process will be beneficial to both you and your students.

The Interview Process

Soon after she graduated from college, my daughter Melanie began looking for a job. I vividly remember a conversation we had after she had taken part in an all-day interview.

"How did it go?" I asked.

"It was interesting. Even though I don't think I want the job, I really want them to offer it to me. Throughout the whole day, I was very aware that I was playing 'the interview game.' Even though everything I said to them was true, I know I phrased things that gave them what they wanted to hear because I wanted to get hired."

"Do you think that's unusual?" I asked.

"I'm not sure," she replied, "but what hit me was that I have never considered myself to be especially competitive, and this was like a competition for me. Even though I can tell you I'm not particularly excited about the job, I know I'll be very disappointed if they don't offer it to me."

Like the rest of us, Melanie is driven in part by a need to be powerful and competent. During the interview process, the picture that drove her was, "What can I say and do to be successful in this situation?" Looked at through such a narrow and specific lens, "success" was defined as being offered a job. As I intimated to Melanie, her behavior was not atypical. A similar "power picture" drove most of us when we began our quest for a job in the field of education. As we sat in a room, facing an interviewer or—even more daunting—an interview team, our immediate objective was to present ourselves in a way that would be looked upon favorably. We spoke honestly but chose our words carefully to impress those who would determine if we would be offered a position.

Most of you reading this book are educators. You obviously presented yourself well enough in your interview to be hired. During the interview process, in all probability there were references made to the school and district mission statements. If you were a well-prepared and savvy candidate, you quite possibly researched the district mission statement and goals. If so, you no doubt looked for opportunities to allude to them in your interview, demonstrating to the interviewer or interviewing team that your beliefs were aligned with those of the district.

There's nothing wrong with any of that. Provided you speak the truth, it only makes sense to present yourself in the most positive way. In fact, such an approach is necessary in a competitive job market. As a school administrator, I admit that a candidate who unobtrusively referenced our goals and mission statement impressed me. It showed me that the candidate cared enough to do some research, and if he or she seemed credible in those statements, it helped me come to the conclusion that we were a good match. For a school and district to be successful, sharing the same vision of quality is essential. Wise applicants are sure to demonstrate that their goals and beliefs are consistent with those held by the district where they hope to work.

For too many of us, however, once the interview is over and the job has been secured, we give little thought to what we want. During the interview, things were clear. We wanted to be hired. Having a clearly identified want made it easy to select the most effective behaviors from an array of possible choices. We need the same clarity of purpose after we have been hired, when we begin our career. As a professional educator, you owe it to yourself to ask the following questions: "What do I want for myself professionally? What are my professional goals?" It's time to interview yourself. It will be the most important interview you will ever have.

WDEP

Bob Wubbolding (1989), director of training for the William Glasser Institute, created a useful tool some years ago called WDEP. Using the call letters of a fictional radio station, WDEP is a mnemonic device that asks you to do the following:

- W: Identify what you *Want*.
- D: Determine what you are *Doing* to achieve your goals.
- E: *Evaluate* your progress.
- P: *Plan* how to maintain your success or improve your performance.

You can use WDEP to develop your professional identity and mission statement. Beyond that, the WDEP process provides a simple, effective way to continually reflect, assess your progress, and plan accordingly. Let's examine WDEP in detail.

W: Want

You *wanted* to be an educator. Now you are one. Although your energy and attention during the hiring process were focused on the goal of becoming an educator, we always have multiple wants in our lives. As soon as we achieve success in one area, other wants come into focus. The wants that make up our internal world are fluid, changing over time as conditions change. Furthermore, we continually prioritize our wants, and not necessarily based on which ones are most important. For example, if you are planning to meet a friend for dinner and find yourself stuck in traffic and delayed, the want that may rise to consciousness is getting to your appointment on time. It's not the most important thing in your life—indeed, it may not be especially important at all—but for the time being, that want dominates your thinking. We all tend to get bogged down by *immediate wants*, even when they are not particularly important. It's easy to get caught up in what Stephen Covey identifies as those things that are "urgent, but not important" (1989, p. 151) and lose sight of the more vital things in life. One of those "vital things" is our professional identity. As an educator, you are continually expected to focus much of your attention on setting up the next parent conference, attending the upcoming staff meeting, getting to your assigned duty period on time, making sure your grades are turned in promptly and accurately, and dealing with the endless bits of "administrivia" that clog our days. While all of these things require your time and attention, if you don't consciously attend to who you want to be as an educator, you can lose sight of the big picture. Your day will be so filled with immediate and pressing issues that it will be easy to forget why you became an educator and what you want from your career.

With that in mind, I invite you to reflect on the following questions. The answers you provide will not be made public. They won't impress an interview team. They are just for you to use to articulate exactly what you expect from your professional career.

- What do you want from yourself as a member of this profession? There will be countless others in the coming years who will be very clear about what they want from you. Put them aside for a minute and identify what kind of educator you want to be and become. While it may be necessary to satisfy the expectations of others, it's more essential that you satisfy your own. What are *yours*?

- Aside from what is written in your school or district mission statement, what is your personal mission statement? It's important to create a mission statement that is congruent with the ideals that your school and district value. Having a shared vision is necessary to achieve the highest-quality education. With that in mind, take your school or district mission statement and personalize it *for you*. Given your current role in the system, what is your personal mission statement, one that supports and promotes the school or district vision? By engaging in this process with reference to the school or district mission statement, you will ensure that your behavior is in alignment with what is valued by the district.

- There are many options for growth within the field of education. Do you want to be/remain a classroom teacher? Do you wish to go into counseling/psychology? Building administration? Central office administration? Become a curriculum specialist? While it is likely that you will develop new wants over your career, it's helpful to have professional goals at any point along your path. Goals need not be lofty or involve "moving up." They can be as simple as "Be the best, most inspiring classroom teacher I can be." If all teachers developed a goal like that and took the time to articulate exactly how we would go about getting there, we would immediately become more "professional" and effective, because we would approach our jobs with greater intentionality, taking a proactive stance rather than continually reacting to the incessant demands that plague teachers.

- When your career is over, how do you wish to be remembered? In today's educational climate, the focus is on improved test scores. I don't expect that fascination to fade away anytime soon. While doing everything you can to ensure your students get a quality educational experience, do you want to be remembered as a teacher whose students "scored the best" on standardized tests? If that is not your most important goal, it would be wise for you to identify how you want to be remembered and begin to create a professional identity that supports your goal while making sure your students perform well. There is considerable talk these days about "accountability." The accountability generally referred to can be neatly summarized on a test report. If you subscribe to a more complex definition of accountability, one that considers the whole child, how will you interact with your students so that you are comfortable being held accountable for the type of men and women they become?

- Until you have a picture of what you *want*, it is hard to develop and sustain motivation and identify the most effective steps to take. Effective action begins with the creation of a dream. What's yours? Dreams need not be grandiose and unrealistic. They can be attainable aspirations. Identifying your professional goals will keep you moving in a positive direction and sustain your professional growth.

While your professional goals will likely evolve and change over time, having a clearly identified, flexible, and dynamic *want* gives you the best chance of becoming the kind of educator you'd like to be. Another trivial example will make my point. Imagine you are at dinner. You have to tell the waiter what you want before you can get it. As long as you remain stuck at, "I'm not sure yet. It all looks so good," you'll never eat! The same is true on a professional level. There are a lot of options. Many of them may "sound delicious," but until you decide which one you want—at least for now—it will be impossible to identify the best steps to take. Take stock. Reflect. Then you will be able to identify your current professional goals and give yourself energy and focus.

D: Doing

In order to achieve what we want, we need to take action. You wanted to become an educator. You did a number of things to become an educator. Considering your current goals, what do you need to do in order to achieve what you want for yourself as a professional?

There are two ways to look at the *doing* aspect of the WDEP process. One is to ask yourself, "What am I currently doing to reach my goals?" This question keeps you focused on the present and your current behaviors. Even with long-term goals, present action is helpful. For example, your long-range goal may be to move into an administrative role, but you are not sure in what capacity. Beginning a costly, time-consuming graduate program at this time may be unwise. That doesn't mean you can't take any action. You are still able to research various administrative roles, have conversations with people in these positions, and begin the process of discovering what role fits most comfortably with who you want to become as a professional. *Doing* includes the research that enables you to take decisive action when the time is right.

It is also prudent to identify things you will need to do in the future. Even if the time is not right to commit to a graduate program now, will you need to complete an intensive program to secure the administrative position you want in the future? Even though you will not need to begin your program of study immediately, you should determine what will be necessary in the future and ask yourself if you are willing to make that commitment. Wanting something is one thing; being committed to taking action to achieve what you want is something very different.

It's not unusual for people to have difficulty getting started and moving toward what they want. Ask yourself the following question: "If I were becoming the educator I would like to be, what steps would I take right now?" Because our nonconscious mind is always working, several potential courses of action will probably present themselves for your consideration. If none of them seems attractive, you may want to reassess your goals or level of commitment.

As you identify those things you can do now and in the future, make a list of possible actions. You don't need to commit to any of them, but having a list that you can refer to will help you stay focused and move toward your goals.

E: Evaluate

The *evaluation* referred to in the WDEP process is *self-evaluation*. As the heart and soul of internal control psychology, self-evaluation invites you to assess yourself honestly. You will continue to be formally evaluated by your supervisors and less formally evaluated by your colleagues and students and parents for the rest of your career. Some of their assessments will be on target; some will be horribly inaccurate, be they positive or negative. Taking responsibility and ownership of your professional life requires you to evaluate yourself.

Remember that effective self-evaluation depends upon both a well-defined picture of what you want and an accurate perception of what is happening. You have to know exactly what you want in order to know if you are being successful. That is why it is necessary that you develop specific goals for yourself. Then, to self-evaluate in a way that promotes growth, you must be completely honest with yourself about how things are going. It may be tempting to paint a picture that is wonderfully positive, but brutal candor is more effective. Forget about all the others who will judge you over the course of your career. Regardless of their perceptions, how satisfied are *you* with your progress? Are you on the road to becoming the kind of educator you want to be? Are you acting in accordance with your values and beliefs? Conscious and intentional self-evaluation, engaged in on a regular basis, will make it easier to act like the person you would like to be.

P: Plan

Regardless of your current level of success, you need to *plan* what to do next. Our plans naturally flow from our evaluation of how well things are going. If you are moving in a positive direction and successfully pursuing your goals, what is your plan to maintain your success? Don't assume that success is self-sustaining. A long-lasting professional career requires ongoing professional development and commitment to those behaviors that perpetuate success.

If you are not experiencing the success you want and not making adequate progress toward your goals, what is your plan to improve?

Rather than wallow in misery when things are going poorly, use the WDEP process to take effective control of your professional life and make plans to have the success you want. While having a clearly defined want is essential, dreams are only realized through action. The most effective action is that which is well planned and well considered.

What makes the WDEP process such a powerful tool is that it ensures that our self-evaluation is conscious. Many people, including professional educators, go through life without full awareness of what they want, what they need to do to succeed, if they are being as successful as they would like, and what plans they should make for future action. The WDEP process allows us to bring intentionality and consciousness to our lives. Well before Wubbolding developed the WDEP process, Greek philosopher Socrates captured its essence in a simple phrase: "The unexamined life is not worth living."

Summary

To be an inspiring teacher, you need a strong professional identity. You have to know what you want and who you want to be. Our need to belong makes it easy to subjugate ourselves when we become part of a larger system. Although it's important for all members of a school and district to work in concert in mutually supportive ways, it is equally important that you create a unique professional identity. Using the WDEP process will help you do that. Most importantly, your students will be better served when you determine the kind of teacher you want to be and take reflective, effective action.

Getting Started

- Use the WDEP process to articulate your professional aspirations and plan of action now. Ask yourself the questions provided in this chapter to begin determining who you want to be and how you will attain your goals.
- Be certain to develop clearly defined goals. Focusing on where you want to be (as opposed to where you currently are) helps

create the motivation needed for effective action. When we create goals for ourselves, we introduce the healthy disequilibrium between what we want and what we have that leads to action. Self-selected professional goals inspire positive action and growth.

- Acting in concert with district goals and expectations, create your own unique goals and professional identity that allow your individuality to emerge. Don't let your desire to "fit in" stop you from bringing forth your unique gifts and talents. Your school and district will be stronger when your individual style flourishes, as long as it is congruent with the district goals.

- Even though you will be evaluated incessantly by others, remember to self-evaluate yourself regularly. Ask: "Am I acting like the educator I would like to be? Am I becoming the educator I want to be?" Even the best external evaluations only capture a snapshot of what you do all day long. Give yourself the professional gift of honest self-evaluation designed to enhance your skills.

Final Thoughts

Our schools are currently in crisis. We are plagued by an alarmingly high dropout rate. And those students who remain in school are often disengaged, acting like little more than enrolled dropouts. While there are pockets of excellence in every school, too many schools are characterized by mediocrity, underperformance, and apathy. Concerned about the welfare of their children, parents are abandoning traditional public schools in increasing numbers, choosing instead to home-educate their children, enroll them in charter schools, or send them to expensive private schools.

There is good news, however. Despite serious problems, we are poised to create a bright future in education. In the recent past, we have made tremendous improvements in our curriculum. The development of state standards has brought about greater instructional consistency, something that promises every child exposure to equal educational opportunity. In today's mobile, shrinking world, we need the uniformity that state standards provide.

Furthermore, professional development initiatives have resulted in improved instructional strategies. Teachers are infinitely better prepared to teach today than they were in years past, and they bring a heightened awareness of the learning objectives they have for students when they begin a lesson. We know so much more about how to teach than we did a generation ago. Still, something is missing.

Despite important and significant advances in curriculum and instruction, our students continue to struggle because we cling to an outdated, obsolete understanding of human motivation. While the mechanistic reward/punishment model might have been adequate when compliance was sufficient, today's world demands a new way to engage and inspire our students. The carrot-and-stick approach, still very much in vogue, has taken us as far as it can. A quality curriculum and sound instructional strategies are of negligible value if students aren't motivated to learn what we are trying to teach. It's time to turn the page.

Fortunately, we can transform our schools and achieve unprecedented success once we start to systematically apply the principles of internal control psychology and implement the practices outlined in this book to enhance student motivation and engagement. It's time to give up our reliance on fear and coercion and instead create need-satisfying classrooms in which teachers and students enjoy positive, productive working relationships. It's time to help our students develop responsibility by giving them opportunities to evaluate themselves routinely. It's time to help them discover they have considerable control over their feelings when they consciously engage in effective actions and thoughts. It's time to help students abandon a victim mentality, where things seem to happen *to* them. Let's teach them that they are largely the architects of their own lives.

It's time to stop complaining that students don't work hard enough and instead help them see that what we teach is relevant to their lives. It's time to offer them demanding challenges, but ones they can meet with reasonable effort. Let's take advantage of the innate desire to learn and create classrooms where every student can experience academic success through sustained effort. When we do this, disruptive behavior will all but disappear, replaced by academic achievement and engagement.

We can do all this. *You* can do all this. But changing how we view student motivation and abandoning the reward/punishment model that we are so familiar and comfortable with take time and conscious thought. It takes commitment. Let me give you an example. Right now, fold your arms across your chest. Switch positions so that the hand that was under one arm is now over it. Feels strange, doesn't it? It's not that hard to do, but unless you give it conscious thought, the next time you fold your arms across your chest, you'll return to the way you have always done things.

The same is true when it comes to understanding student motivation and the practices advocated in this book. Initially, they seem relatively simple to understand and apply. But unless you remain conscious and intentional, you will return to a reward/punishment orientation almost immediately, even if you agree with everything I have proposed. Long-term habits are hard to break—but they can be broken and replaced with more effective new behaviors.

The solution? Stay focused. Stay aware. Use the WDEP process to help you regularly assess what you want and what you need to do to keep moving in a positive direction. Make transforming your classroom and creating an inspiring school your priority. When you develop the mind-set that you are committed to the concepts of internal motivation and control, you will be on your way. Others have made this decision and experienced deep professional satisfaction and success. Your school can achieve as much or more. By implementing the practices suggested in this book, you can transform your school, inspire your students, and take full advantage of the recent improvements in curriculum and instruction. We owe it to ourselves and to our students to create schools and classrooms that bring out the best in the next generation.

References

Armstrong, T. (2006). *The best schools: How human development research should inform educational practice.* Alexandria, VA: ASCD.

Chaddock, G. (2006, June 21). U.S. high school dropout rate: High, but how high? *Christian Science Monitor.* Available: http://www.csmonitor.com/2006/0621/p03s02-ussc.html

Covey, S. (1989). *The 7 habits of highly effective people: Powerful lessons in personal change.* New York: Simon & Schuster.

Dillon, S. (2008, March 20). States' data obscure how few finish high school. *New York Times.* Available: http://www.nytimes.com/2008/03/20/education/20graduation.html.

Erwin, J. (2004). *The classroom of choice: Giving students what they need and getting what you want.* Alexandria, VA: ASCD.

Glasser, W. (1984). *Control theory: A new explanation of how we control our lives.* New York: Harper & Row.

Glasser, W. (1990). *The quality school: Managing students without coercion.* New York: HarperCollins.

Glasser, W. (1998). *Choice theory: A new psychology of personal freedom.* New York: HarperCollins.

Graham, M. (2007). *Leadership that reaches every student: A guide for teachers and parents who are concerned about providing students with vision and leadership.* Lincoln, NE: iUniverse.

Hargis, C. (1995). *Curriculum based assessment: A primer.* Springfield, IL: Charles C. Thomas.

Jensen, E. (1998). *Teaching with the brain in mind.* Alexandria, VA: ASCD.

Kohn, A. (1993). *Punished by rewards: The trouble with gold stars, incentive plans, A's, praise, and other bribes.* Boston: Houghton Mifflin.

Leachman, G., & Victor, D. (2003). Student-led class meetings. *Educational Leadership, 60*(6), 64–68.

Marzano, R. (2007). *The art and science of teaching: A comprehensive framework for effective instruction.* Alexandria, VA: ASCD.

Marzano, R., & Marzano, J. (2003). The key to classroom management. *Educational Leadership, 61*(1), 6–13.

May, R. (1953). *Man's search for himself.* New York: Norton.

National Commission on Excellence in Education. (1983). *A nation at risk.* Washington, DC: GPO. Available: http://www.ed.gov/pubs/NatAtRisk/index.html

Saphier, J., & Gower, R. (1997). *The skillful teacher: Building your teaching skills.* Acton, MA: Research for Better Teaching.

Schaps, E. (2003). Creating a school community. *Educational Leadership, 60*(6), 31–33.

Schmoker, M. (2006). *Results now: How we can achieve unprecedented improvements in teaching and learning.* Alexandria, VA: ASCD.

Sullo, R. (2007). *Activating the desire to learn.* Alexandria, VA: ASCD.

Sullo, R. (2008). *The inspiring teacher: Making a positive difference in students' lives.* Annapolis, MD: NEA Profess ional Library.

Tate, M. (2004). *Sit and get won't grow dendrites: Twenty learning strategies that engage the adult brain.* Thousand Oaks, CA: Corwin Press.

Tomlinson, C. (1999). *The differentiated classroom: Responding to the needs of all learners.* Alexandria, VA: ASCD.

Tomlinson, C. (2003). *Fulfilling the promise of the differentiated classroom: Strategies and tools for responsive teaching.* Alexandria, VA: ASCD.

Tomlinson, C., & McTighe, J. (2006). *Integrating differentiated instruction and Understanding by Design.* Alexandria, VA: ASCD.

Turque, B. (2008, November 2). Incentives can make or break students. *Washington Post.* Available: http://www.washingtonpost.com/wpdyn/content/article/2008/11/01/AR2008110101989.html

Westwater, A., & Wolfe, P. (2000). The brain-compatible curriculum. *Educational Leadership, 58*(3), 49–52.

Wong, H., & Wong, R. (1998). *The first days of school: How to be an effective teacher.* Mountain View, CA: Harry K. Wong Publications.

Wubbolding, R. (1989, Spring). Radio station WDEP and other metaphors used in teaching reality therapy. *Journal of Reality Therapy, 8*(2), 74–79.

Index

note: page numbers followed by *f* refer to figures.

About the Author

During his 33 years as an educator, Bob Sullo worked as an English teacher, a school psychologist, an adjustment counselor, and an administrator in the Plymouth Public Schools in Plymouth, Massachusetts. These diverse roles gave him the opportunity to work in both regular education and special education, serving students from prekindergarten through graduation in elementary, middle, and high school.

Currently an educational consultant and instructor for the William Glasser Institute, Bob has provided staff development and parent workshops in more than 30 states. His presentations focus on internal motivation, responsibility, and the creation of a positive environment where students are inspired to produce high-quality academic work. Bob's previous books include *Teach Them to Be Happy* (New View Publications, 1989), *Inspiring Quality in Your School: From Theory to Practice* (NEA Professional Library, 1997), *Activating the Desire to Learn* (ASCD, 2007), *Managing to Inspire: Bringing Out the Best in Those You Supervise* (iUniverse, 2007), and *The Inspiring Teacher: Making a Positive Difference in Students' Lives* (NEA Professional Library, 2008).

Bob can be reached at P.O. Box 1336, Sandwich, MA 02563. For training or consulting, visit Bob's Web site at www.internal motivation.net or e-mail him at bob@internalmotivation.net.

Related ASCD Resources: Motivating Students

At the time of publication, the following ASCD resources were available; for the most up-to-date information about ASCD resources, go to www. ascd.org. ASCD stock numbers are noted in parentheses.

Books

Activating the Desire to Learn, by Bob Sullo (#107009S25)

Activating and Engaging Habits of Mind, by Arthur L. Costa and Bena Kallick (#100033S25)

The Big Picture: Education Is Everyone's Business, by Dennis Littky and Samantha Grabelle (#104438S25)

Multimedia

Emotional Intelligence Professional Inquiry Kit, by Pam Robbins and Jane Scott (#997146S25)

Project-Based Learning with Multimedia (CD-ROM), by the San Mateo County Office of Education (#502117S25)

Video

High Schools at Work: Creating Student-Centered Learning Three Tape Series with Facilitator's Guide (#406117S25)

Educating Everybody's Children, Tape 4: Increasing Interest, Motivation, and Engagement (#400225S25)

The Whole Child Initiative helps schools and communities create learning environments that allow students to be healthy, safe, engaged, supported, and challenged. To learn more about other books and resources that relate to the whole child, visit www.wholechildeducation.org.

For more information, visit us on the World Wide Web (http://www.ascd. org), send an e-mail message to member@ascd.org, call the ASCD Service Center (1-800-933-ASCD or 703-578-9600, then press 2), send a fax to 703-575-5400, or write to Information Services, ASCD, 1703 N. Beauregard St., Alexandria, VA 22311-1714 USA.